OUT OF CONTROL:

Apocalyptic Psychology in the Age of Trump

Richard Kradin, M.D.

ISBN-10:0692091610
ISBN-13;9780692091616

About the Author:

Richard Kradin is a physician at the Massachusetts General Hospital, a psychoanalyst with certification in both psychoanalysis and Jungian analysis and professor at Harvard Medical School. He is the former Research Director of the Mind-Body Medical Institute at Harvard. He holds graduate degrees in Chemical Physics and Religion. He is the recipient of the *Small Prize* (summa cum laude) from Harvard (Religion) and the *Gradiva Award* for best paper in psychoanalysis. Dr. Kradin is the author of more than 200 articles in the scientific literature and six textbooks including the *Herald Dream* (Karnac), *The Placebo Response* (Routledge), *Pathologies of the Mind-Body Interface* (Routledge), and the *Parting the Ways: Esoteric Judaism in the Psychologies of Freud and Jung* (Academic Studies Press). He lectures in the U.S. and internationally. He maintains a private practice in psychoanalysis in Boston, MA.

Dedication:

This book is dedicated to friends, colleagues, and family who recognize the continued importance of free speech in America.

Contents

Preface

This book has been a long time in the making. It is the formulation of my ideas about the psychology of what is currently transpiring in America. America is at a crossroads, and its future success or decline will depend on whether its citizens are sufficiently informed about what is driving the current conflicts in society.

I was a college student in the 1960s and participated in the domestic protests of that time. For most of my adult life, I considered myself to be a liberal-minded Democratic voter. But as Ronald Reagan famously remarked, "I didn't leave the Democratic Party, the Democratic Party left me." Progressivism today has aligned itself with issues and tactics that I cannot relate to, and that threaten to rend the fabric of American society.

The French jurist Anselme Batbie once remarked, "He who is not a liberal at age twenty compels one to doubt the generosity of his heart, but he who persists in this way of thinking after age thirty, compels one to doubt the soundness of his mind." I am well past thirty and keenly aware that change can appear misguided when it no longer comports with one's established ways of thinking. However, I truly believe that even as a young man, I would have found repugnant much of what I see transpiring in America today. I find the politically correct agenda, the deterioration of journalistic standards, the ready access to pornography, the growing divide between rich and poor in this country, and the addictive aspects of social media, all deeply disturbing. The level of enmity and disrespect exhibited by all sides of the political spectrum is unprecedented in my lifetime, and I can see little that is redeeming in it.

As a psychoanalyst trained to discern the phenomenology of psychopathology, I have grown increasingly convinced that Americans—especially those on the Progressive left—are succumbing to neurotic obsessional and quasi-delusional modes of thought. This psychological transformation has been slowly developing over the last half century and corresponds temporally to the ascendancy of feminism and the civil rights movement. But it has accelerated and taken on a toxic quality due to social pressures mediated by high-speed digital technologies.

The present text is my effort to bring my knowledge of psychology and comparative religion to address what I think is transpiring today. I hope that the reader will glean something from my efforts.

Acknowledgements

I would like to thank S., my family, friends, and colleagues, for serving as a sounding board for my ideas and for reading this manuscript.

Introduction:
America in Conflict

I'm truly sorry man's dominion,
Has broken nature's social union.

—Robert Burns, To a Mouse

America is undergoing a series of rapid transformations. With the emergence of global markets, long-term job security is no longer assured. There is an increase in violent crimes in some major urban areas. Unpredictable acts of random terror have occurred in our schools and on our streets, and the threat of nuclear disaster looms ever present. These changes have not made Americans more secure, and, unsurprisingly, many citizens report states of heightened anxiety.

The political and cultural positions of Americans are currently highly polarized. Legislators in Washington appear to be incapable of finding common ground. Historically, internecine conflicts have occurred before when people hold rigidly polarized unwavering positions. The present situation in America shares features with what religious scholars refer to as *apocalyptic* imagination (Collins, 1984). Most people today think of an *apocalypse* as the catastrophic destruction that will bring the world to an end. But the term is Greek for *revelation*. Although there was a foreboding element in the ancient apocalyptic thought, it had other defining features. The term is used by scholars today in two distinct ways. One refers to the ideology (i.e., a way of thinking), the other as the literary form that was common in the intertestamental period (i.e., between the closing of the Old Testament and the appearance of the New Testament, when these writings flourished). What is common to apocalyptic thought, and which will be discussed in greater detail, is a rigid psychological perspective that categorizes people as either "Good" or "Evil." In modern terms, this is what psychiatrists would refer to as obsessional black-and-white thinking.

The founders of psychoanalysis, and subsequently *social* psychologists, displayed a keen interest in the dialectic between the individual and factors that may be prevalent in society. A great deal has been written in recent years concerning America's culture wars and political conflicts, and most of this has been written by social scientists. Curiously, few have addressed the underlying factors that foster divisiveness from the perspective of depth psychology (Schwarz, 2003). Yet as the early psychoanalyst Carl Jung suggested, no Archimedean point exists outside of the human psyche by which to assess *any* topic. All human endeavors are ultimately psychological ones and therefore should properly, although not necessarily exclusively, be examined through that lens.

The aim of this text is to examine the underlying rigid psychological positions that are driving conflict in America today. It will be argued that America has witnessed a marked increase in obsessional ideation and behaviors. In its current form, it is an expression of an ancient apocalyptic myth that pits Americans against each other and resists compromise.

Although psychologists are best trained to analyze these issues, as a group they are not without their own political and cultural biases. As the social psychologist has demonstrated, American psychologists today hold political views that are well to the left of center. A recent article in *Scientific American* addresses this finding (Valdassalo, 2015):

> Does Social Psychology need more political diversity? Here's one thing on which everyone can agree: social psychology is overwhelmingly composed of liberals (around 85%). The question of why this is the case, and whether it presents a problem for the field, is more controversial. The topic has exploded out of our conference halls and into major news outlets over the past several years, with claims of both overt hostility and subtle bias against conservative students, colleagues, and their publications, being met with reactions ranging from knee-jerk dismissal to sincere self-reflection and measured methodological critique.

The liberal bias of psychotherapists is not new, but it has in recent years become more extreme, for reasons that might best be addressed elsewhere in a text devoted to the history of the psychotherapy movement. But the fact is that few clinical psychologists today espouse or tolerate conservative views. Many react to them with hostility, which is odd for a field based on the invitation to express one's thoughts freely, without fear of being criticized.

Attempting a psychological analysis of society, with its cultural and political complexities, is a complex task. For one thing, psychology is not a "hard" science; instead, it is subject to suggestion, which means that people unwittingly but necessarily influence the thoughts and behaviors of others. But when factions in a society hold highly opposing views, this influence generally manifests as an "allergic" reaction. How, then, is one to determine whose perspective is correct? Some psychologists would argue that all perspectives are equally valid and therefore beyond being challenged. This position is an indication of how far the field of psycho-therapy has strayed from its origins. The inescapable truthis that clinical psychologists are constantly making moral judgments in their role, even if they do not express them or *imagine* that they are free of bias (London, 1986).

At a societal level, highly polarized perspectives result in dysfunction. Consider an individual who is psychologically highly conflicted. It is easy to recognize that such an individual will be unable to act effectively. This is the cardinal feature of neurosis, and it is true as well of a society at odds with itself.

For this reason, the present attempt at elucidating the psychology of today's society will apply several criteria to determine the legitimacy of the conflicted positions. Admittedly, others might choose a different set of criteria, but the ones adopted here were chosen to achieve clarity. They include the following:

(1) Are the perspectives presented by the opposing societal factions in America today based primarily on facts or beliefs? Facts are the basis

for scientific observations; beliefs are not. It is not possible to argue with someone's beliefs. As will be discussed, people also argue about facts, but in the end facts speak for themselves. For example, if a statistical study shows, let's say, results X, scientists may legitimately argue about whether X was the result of faulty experimental design or bias. How to interpret X can also be debated, but the facts, unless falsified, cannot be denied.

(2) Are the positions adopted by the opposing factions rational, and, just as important, can they be shown to be effective in a positive way? This is a pragmatic approach. I have addressed this question elsewhere in a text on the placebo effect, in which people respond to drugs or interventions that by themselves are known to be ineffective (R. Kradin, 2008). It turns out that many rational and commonsensical therapeutic approaches prove to be ineffective. A current example may be the arguments for gun control. At first glance, it does seem to make good sense that limiting access to guns should improve homicide rates in America. But the evidence does not support that conclusion, because there are many other factors that contribute to the result. Criminals may find ways to obtain guns illegally, for example. Nevertheless, it remains a hotly contested issue in America because some refuse to *believe* that gun control can be ineffective. Not every rational idea is necessarily a good one.

(3) Finally, do the positions and behaviors exhibited by the opposing factions in America meet psychiatric criteria for an accepted psychopathology? Psychopathology is always a sign of distorted perspectives. Although it may sound odd to suggest that large numbers of Americans today might be suffering from signs of mental illness, there is compelling evidence to suggest that this is the case, at least with respect to how they view certain issues in society.

These criteria will be applied to the present analysis in the spirit of psychoanalysis, which is not primarily to judge, but to elucidate. Nevertheless, it is impossible to conduct a psychoanalysis that is devoid of values, and these will be thoroughly discussed (London, 1986).

Chapter 1:
Two Visions of America

Until recently, Americans in general shared a common set of values: love of nation, love of family, respect for freedom of religious expression and freedom of speech, and confidence in the moral goodness of the country. These defined the American spirit at home and in the eyes of much of the world. But this is changing, and the reasons merit analysis.

Jung suggested that man is a *mythopoetic* creature (i.e., that the human psyche is innately myth producing) and that individuals and societies tend to be guided along the paths of a limited number of innate psychological motifs. These myths are not "fictions" as we commonly think of them today. Instead, they are manifestations of an *a priori* ordering of experience that occurs automatically within the psyche via what Jung referred to as *archetypes.* These *archetypes* are transpersonal and shared by all people in what he referred to as the *collective unconscious.*[1] According to Jung:

> The collective unconscious appears to consist of mythological motifs or primordial images, for which reason the myths of all nations are its real exponents. In fact, the whole of mythology could be taken as a sort of projection of the collective unconscious.... These influences are nothing but unconscious introspective perceptions of the collective unconscious. (C. G. Jung, 1998)

Jung was keenly aware of the role of myth and the potential neg-

---

1   The notion of the collective unconscious is fundamental to Jung's psychology. Like Plato's notion of the archetypes and the Kantian a priori, Jung argued that human psychology was bounded and predisposed to creating images that, although varied, were limited so that comparable mythic motifs recur in diverse populations. Frazer's Golden Bough was an early anthropological effort at collecting and comparing these myths based on specific and limited themes.

ative effects that unconscious forces can impose on societies. He argued that it is critical to discern the guiding myth(s) of a society if one is to identify its likely trajectory. Furthermore, when there are prevalent competing myths within a society, conflict will invariably develop until one becomes clearly dominant (C. G. Jung, 1950). In America today, two opposing mythic visions are nearly equally prevalent, and the result is the conflict that we are witnessing.

Opposing myths have been common in man's history (Stoyanov, 2000). They were seen in ancient Egypt as the opposing wills of the gods Seth and Osiris, in the Zoroastrian struggle of the ancient gods Ohrmazd and Ahriman, and the antagonism of the Greek gods Apollo and Dionysius. These are examples of what has been termed *radical duality*. As the religious historian Yuri Stoyanov wrote:

> Dualist religions in antiquity sought to redefine often radically the interrelationships between the divine, human, and natural worlds, commonly by identifying the source of evil in a force or forces in the divine and supernatural worlds. (Stoyanov, 2000 p. xi)

For Jung, a student of comparative religion, these dualistic systems were in fact expressions of how the human psyche was structured as archetypal *opposites*, so that opposing visions were not limited to antiquity but instead fated to reemerge in all times. As he notes (C. G. Jung, 1962):

> We think we can congratulate ourselves on having already reached such a pinnacle of clarity, imagining that we have left all these phantasmal gods far behind. But what we have left behind are only verbal specters, not the psychic facts that were responsible for the birth of the gods. We are still as much possessed today by autonomous psychic contents as if they were Olympians. Today they are called phobias, obsessions, and so forth; in a word, neurotic symptoms. The gods have become diseases. (Jung, *Golden Flower*, para. 254)

Today we refer to these motifs as neuroses, but essentially nothing has changed since ancient times.

Unconstrained and Constrained Mythic Visions

The conservative political commentator Thomas Sowell has argued in *Conflict of Visions* that Americans are at odds concerning what constitutes the greatest "good" in society (Sowell, 2007). Like Jung, he argues that their "visions" are driven by unconscious factors subject to "what we sense or feel before we have constructed any systematic reasoning that could be called a theory, much less … a hypotheses to be tested against evidence" (Sowell, 2007) p. 4).

Sowell suggests that the opposing mythic visions are prone to intensify during times of societal upheaval. He terms them the *constrained* and *unconstrained visions*, a political reimagining of the Apollonian and Dionysian perspectives of order and disorder, and these terms will be adopted throughout the present text. Phenomenologically, they influence a range of issues that tend to cluster around a mythic core. According to Sowell:

> One of the curious things about political opinions is how often the same people line up on opposite sides of different issues. The issues themselves may have no intrinsic connection with each other. They may range from military spending to drug laws to monetary policy to education. Yet the same familiar faces can be found glaring at each other from opposite sides of the political fence, again and again. It happens too often to be a coincidence and it is too uncontrolled to be a plot. (Sowell, *Visions*, p. 3)

The *constrained vision* values collective wisdom or what might loosely be termed "common sense." It was the prevailing view in the earliest civilizations of Egyptian, Babylonian, and ancient Israel. New ideas, religions,[2] and novel individual contributions, unlike today, were all suspect within ancient hierarchical societies. Indeed, authors in antiquity chose to

---

2   In the first century CE, Judaism was accepted as an official religion and exempt from honoring the Roman Gods. On the other hand, early Christians were persecuted for "atheism," as it was considered a "new" religion and therefore lacking in esteem. This would change in the fourth century with Constantine's adoption of Christianity as the state religion.

publish their works pseudonymously rather than claim ideas as their own, as accepted wisdom was more likely to find a large audience.

The *constrained vision* structures the society via law and rituals. Sigmund Freud argued that law emerged in the ancient world to counter the instinctual, pleasure-seeking behaviors of individuals (Freud & Strachey, 1989). They aimed at protecting lives and property from those inclined to take what was not their own. This conflict between man's desires and society's security is part of man's inheritance as both an omnivorous animal and a social primate. Freud quotes the opinion of anthropologist James Frazer in *Totem and Taboo*:

"The law only forbids men to do what their instincts incline them to do; what nature itself prohibits and punishes, it would be superfluous for the law to prohibit and punish. Accordingly, we may always safely assume that crimes forbidden by law are crimes which many men have a natural propensity to commit." (Frazier, quoted in Freud, *Totem,* p. 204)

The *constrained* vision focuses on *chronos*, or the cyclical nature of time. Most ancient civilizations marked time by either a lunar cycle or a mixed lunar-solar calendar. As natural events repeated themselves with regularity (e.g., the cycles of the moon, the seasons, the flooding of major rivers, etc.), genuine novelty was judged impossible. Sources of wisdom were also considered fixed, as when Ecclesiastes 1:9 suggests that there is "nothing new under the sun." Whereas new technologies did develop in ancient times, they did so at a far slower rate than today.

The Unconstrained Vision

In contrast to the conservative attitudes of the Near East, the *unconstrained vision* appears to have emerged historically in ancient Greece, which for reasons uncertain tended to value the accomplishments of men above that of the collective. A pantheon of anthropomorphic Greek gods played favorites with men of valor, or heroes, as evidenced from Homer's *Iliad*. Excellence was man's primary virtue. As early as the fifth century

BCE, the sophist Protagoras proclaimed that "Man is the measure of all things."

His contemporary Socrates questioned what his fellow Athenians knew about the values that constituted a "good" life. What we know of Socrates' ideas were transmitted in the writings of his two students, Plato and Xenophon. [3] In the *Republic*, Plato argues that governing should be left to men who are rational and intelligent (i.e., philosophers like himself) (Bloom, 2016). Democracy—in which all men regardless of their capacities would participate directly in their own governance was, according to Plato, a prescription for chaos that would ultimately lead to tyranny. He wrote:

The society (democracy) we have described can never grow into a reality or see the light of day, and there will be no end to the troubles of states, or indeed, my dear Glaucon, of humanity itself, till philosophers become rulers in this world, or till those we now call kings and rulers really and truly become philosophers, and political power and philosophy thus come into the same hands. (Plato, *Republic*, p. 138; parenthetical addition mine)

Plato was an idealist. This meant that he viewed the physical world as an imperfect representation of supernal *archetypes* and that only the latter was immutable and therefore ontologically "real." The material world was a crude copy of the *archetypes*, and unlike the latter it was subject both to change and decay. Man's soul, according to Plato, was derived from a supernal realm and was trapped temporarily in a bodily prison, but yearned to be restored to its proper location in the spiritual realm. This idea would over time permeate all the monotheistic religions due to influence of Hellenism beginning in the fourth century BCE.

Unlike his teacher Plato, Aristotle, who would with time exert an immense influence on medieval religious philosophy, was an empiricist

---

3   Like many wise men of the time, Socrates wrote nothing that is currently extant. Instead, we know his thoughts through the writings of his student Plato. As in all such scenarios, it is impossible to glean the thoughts of Socrates from Plato's own.

whose focus was directed primarily at earthly matters. He was in many respects a Greek champion of the *constrained vision*. His writings were extensive and ranged from both physical to metaphysical topics. In *The School of Athens,* Raphael's famous fresco, which can still be viewed today in the Apostolic Palace of the Vatican, Plato is portrayed with his finger pointing toward the sky while Aristotle's hand is extended toward the ground. The image poses the eternal question: How are the ideal and the real to be reconciled? It is the question that currently plagues America.

Human Nature

The *unconstrained vision* imagines human nature as ultimately perfectible, and this forms the basis for its ideal of moral progress. From the *unconstrained vision,* man is expected to evolve to ever higher states of moral rectitude, and the laws of society must change in parallel if they are to remain aligned with progress.

As Sowell suggests, in today's America, what are referred to as *Progressives*—virtually all members of the present Democratic Party and a smaller number of Republicans—are guided primarily by the *unconstrained vision* on matters of morality.[4] They see no higher calling than moral progress. For example, they consider the U.S. Constitution to be a "living document," one that is subject to change via Progressive interpretation.

In contrast, Conservatives today—most Republicans and few Democrats—are guided by the *constrained vision*. They hold that the nation's laws can only be changed by the acts of legislation and by the electorate, as prescribed in the Constitution. Via argument and compromise, the Founding Fathers devised a separation of powers between the legislative,

---

4   Throughout this text, the term *liberal Progressive* can be roughly equated with the Democratic Party, and *Conservative* with the Republican Party. Although in the past this was overly general, the polarization of American polity closely follows this conclusion as can be confirmed by an examination of the political platforms espoused by the Democratic and Republican parties in the recent 2016 presidential election.

executive, and judicial branches of the new American government that was designed to inhibit the interests of any single group within society. While the Founders were men of their time, they made specific efforts to envision how circumstances might change in the future and designed a system that was sufficiently flexible to meet those demands.

Conservatives tend to be "strict constructivists" who maintain that because the values of the Founding Fathers were cautiously reasoned, they remain applicable now and in the future. For them, the U.S. Constitution approximates holy "scripture," to be interpreted but not changed without reasoned consideration and the consent of the people. A recent example of this conflict of *visions* in America has been the so-called Trump Travel Ban. The Constitution specifically invests the president, as the chief executive of the country, with the power to determine the limits of immigration in times of perceived national threat. When the executive branch issued a recent travel ban, claiming that immigration from several failed nation states might constitute a security risk for the legal entry of terrorists, injunctions against the ban were issued by several Progressive federal judges. Ultimately, the U.S. Supreme Court, finely balanced between Conservative and Progressive justices, and citing the president's constitutional authority, upheld the travel ban (Liptak, 2017).

The *constrained vision* holds that man is naturally prone to selfishness and greed and cannot be relied upon to police himself with respect to the rights and possessions of others. Differences between individuals are viewed as representations of the heterogeneity of the species. The idea of genuine equality between men is not supported by empirical observation and is judged naive.

The *constrained vision* is a pragmatic one. It reasons that as man is imperfect and necessarily flawed and that societal safeguards are proper to safeguard against those who might be inclined to violate the rights and property of others with impunity. This view is explicated in the Hebrew Bible, which details in Exodus 21-23 the civil laws and punishments required to preserve the fabric of society.

However, some interpret this as what the French philosopher Paul Ricoeur termed a "dark view" of human,nature, one the he attributed to Freud, Marx, and Nietzsche (Sims, 2003). Freud did suggest that innate unconscious drives needed to be restrained by rules in the process of socialization. The structure of psychoanalysis, what he referred to as its "framework," was conceived by Freud to contain the unconscious impulses of both the patient and the analyst, thereby protecting the integrity of the treatment (R. Kradin, 2016). Such safeguards run like fractal derivatives throughout the meta-theory and rituals of classical psychoanalysis and many of its derivatives. The social commentator Phillip Rieff writes, "On the whole Freud stands with Hobbes as opposed to Rousseau; not that man is good and society corrupts him, but that man is anarchic and society restrains him" (Rieff, 1979) p. 221). As efforts at self-restraint cannot be relied upon, some men can be expected to aggress against others should the opportunity arise. Indeed, Freud's opinions of his fellow man were far from complimentary:

> [M]en are not gentle creatures who want to be loved, and who at the most can defend themselves if attacked; they are, on the contrary, creatures among whose instinctual endowments are to be reckoned a powerful share of aggressiveness. Thus, their neighbor is for them not only a potential helper or sexual object but also someone who tempts them to satisfy their aggressiveness on him, to exploit his capacity for work without compensation, to use him sexually without his consent, to seize his possessions, to humiliate him, to cause him pain, to torture and kill him. *Homo homini lupus*. (Freud, *Civilization*, p. 58)

Anthropologists like Colin Turnbull have noted that the moral veneer of civil society quickly vanishes in times of war, disease, and famine. When the necessities of life are scarce, studies suggest, few can be counted on to behave generously toward others. Indeed, they may instead exhibit frank malevolence, even toward near kin (R. Kradin, 1999). Morality is a thin layer in the cognitive framework of highly evolved human minds, but it is susceptible to rapid erosion in times of limited resources, when man is driven primarily by Darwin's bestial law of the survival of the fittest.

From the perspective of the *constrained vision,* transforming human nature is not simply difficult, it is nearly impossible, and there is good biological and experiential evidence to support this view. From a neurobiological perspective, character reflects the repeated conditioning of neurons in the central nervous system over the course of a lifetime. When the same neural pathways are utilized over and over, their synaptic connections become functionally stronger. This yields "structures" that are resistant to change (R. L. Kradin, 2004). Character—or personality, if one prefers—is such a structure. It is also our greatest source of "addiction." Although rarely discussed as such in the clinical psychology literature, we are all addicted to who we are. Consequently, efforts at change are met with defenses, anxiety, and resistance. Only with sustained consistent effort, what Freud described as "working through," is mutative change likely to occur. Indeed, Rabbi Israel Salanter, who was the leader of the nineteenth-century pre-psychoanalytical Mussar movement, famously remarked that it was easier to memorize the entire Talmud (a massive tome) than to make any change in one's character.

From a scientific perspective, the perfectibility of human nature, which is an integral aspect of the *unconstrained vision,* is an "ideal." It is questionable whether someone who has broken the law will on their own can be expected to behave well in the future.[5] Indeed, one of the potential concerns with the process of psychotherapy, when practiced by the vast majority of clinicians who hold the *unconstrained vision,* is their potential unwillingness to prognosticate concerning the likelihood of therapeutic change, because to do so would deny the possibility of perfectibility. In such cases, psychotherapeutic treatments can become interminable. On the other hand, to be overly pessimistic concerning the potential for change is to succumb to nontherapeutic nihilism. As in most cases, the optimal approach is the "middle path."

---

5   Donald Trump has, at several rallies, read the lyrics of the Al Wilson ballad "The Snake," which alludes to the observation that some ill-intentioned people cannot be expected to change their way of being. It is a highly puerile rendition, but its lesson is sound.

Time and Memory

Those who hold the *unconstrained vision* tend to see progress as the result of the passage of *linear* time, with time's arrow serving as a "metronome."[6] According to the pre-Socratic Greek philosopher Heraclitus, "No man steps into the *same* river twice." From this perspective stasis is impossible, and even the repetition of natural events is never *exactly* the same. History too is judged to be contextual and in continual flux. From this perspective, past events have limited relevance in a changing world.

It follows that memory, which represents recollections of the past, also is attributed limited value from the *unconstrained vision*. Progress has a "short memory." Today change occurs with such rapidity that time is experienced as contracted. Events that occupied the airwaves one day are rapidly replaced by new ones and quickly forgotten. The *unconstrained vision* resists the influence of what is old and "outdated." The psychoanalyst Wilfred Bion affirmed this idea in his suggestion that each new therapy session is best approached "without memory or desire" (Bion, 1967). Bion's point was that memory can potentially foreclose on the emergence of new possibilities. But is this truly good advice? Perhaps more to the point, is it possible?[7] In the absence of memory, it is impossible to construct any meaningful narrative. Events remain disconnected, and there can be no indication of what is likely to occur in the future.

Memory is at the very core of our being. Indeed, it can be convincingly argued that we *are* our memories. Can you imagine waking each day, like Phil Connors in the movie *Groundhog Day,* and having to repeat the same day over and over? But in that film, the protagonist takes the op-

---

6   The monotheistic religions include a concept of the beginning and ending of time, so that there is a recognized progression. However, by adopting a calendar that is determined both by the sun and moon, Judaism maintains the notion of circular *chronos* that is not common to Christianity. Islam maintains a purely lunar calendar, and it is tempting to suggest that the absence of a solar contribution to the calendar has limited progress in the Islamic world.

7   It is noteworthy that Bion spent part of his childhood in India, where he was exposed to aspects of Hindu meditative traditions that promote similar concepts.

portunity to remember and to learn from his oft-repeated experiences. He improves himself, and that cannot be achieved without memory.

Attitudes toward remembering have had an enormous influence on politics and society. The philosopher George Santayana opined, "Those who cannot remember the past are condemned to repeat it." From the perspective of the *constrained vision*, to ignore the past is foolhardy. The recent movie *Darkest Hour* portrays Winston Churchill's response to his political opponents who plead with him to begin peace negotiations with Hitler to avoid the invasion of England by German troops. Churchill angrily chides them by reminding them of the dreadful results when they last attempted to negotiate peace with the German leader at Munich in 1936. Failures to remember can have disastrous consequences.

Ignorance of the past and the devaluation of memory can yield neurotic disjunctions within both individuals and societies. As Freud noted, "repetition compulsion," the tendency to repeat past behaviors in view of their past lack of success, is a cardinal feature of neurosis. His perspective may reflect his Jewish heritage (R. Kradin, 2016). In *Zachor*—the Hebrew imperative "Remember!"—the Israeli historian Yosef Hayyim Yerushalmi describes how collective memories were traditionally re-worked in Judaism (Yerushalmi, 1996). This is comparable to Freud's theory of how memories are re-transcribed in the process of recollecting them in the present (*nachtraglikheit*). Remembering is necessary if individuals and societies are to avoid danger. As I am writing this, the country has witnessed yet another fatal mass shooting in an American school. Yet nothing of substance has been done to reduce the risk of these massacres occurring in the future. This is not simply a political issue; rather it constitutes a resistance to remembering and thereby learning from the past and properly adapting. Following a merciless attack by the Amalekites on the old and feeble Israelites who were fleeing Egypt, the Book of Exodus states:

God said to Moses: "Write this as a remembrance in the Book and recite it in the ears of Joshua, that I shall surely erase the memory of Amalek from under the heavens…and Moses said, "God maintains a war against

Amalek from generation to generation." (Exodus 17)

The message is that existential dangers have existed and likely always will exist in this world. They should not be forgotten. Indeed, what is best remembered versus forgotten constitutes a challenge for any society and an aspect of the conflict between its guiding *visions*. Yet if the criteria set out for assessing the relative value of the opposing views is applied, it must be concluded that real progress includes a realistic assessment and remembering of past behaviors.

Seeking Truth

The conflicts between visions raise profound questions as to what constitutes truth, as those who hold to the *constrained* and *unconstrained* *visions* are unable to agree on an answer. The very idea of "truth" as it was traditionally known is under siege today, a fact confirmed by recent behavioral research. In the *Post Truth Era*, the psychologist Ralph Keyes suggests that lying with impunity is currently a widespread phenomenon in America (Keyes, 2016). The adage "Honesty is the best policy" no longer holds. Instead, Keynes suggests, telling the "truth" has been replaced by what passes as "believable." The cause of this post-modern decline in truth-telling is undoubtedly complex, and no single explanation will likely suffice, but there is evidence that it parallels a decline in religious values. Ingrid Storm, a researcher at the University of Manchester, showed that religious people do, in fact, disapprove more strongly of breaches of truth than those who are nonreligious, although the degree of difference was less than for other societal issues (e.g., views concerning sexuality) (Storm, 2015).

The former Chief Rabbi of Great Britain, Sir Jonathan Sacks, describes the research results of the experimental psychologist Aza Norenzayan (Norenzayan, 2013) in an essay on the role of religion and morality in society as follows:

A whole series of experiments has shed light on the role of religious practice.... Tests have been carried out in which participants have the opportunity to cheat and gain by so doing. If, without any connection being made to the experiment at hand, participants have been primed (subliminally) to thin religious thoughts—by being shown words relating to God, for example, or being reminded of the Ten Commandments—they cheat significantly less. What is particularly fascinating about such tests is that outcomes show no relationship to the underlying beliefs of the participants. (Sacks, 2016, p. 135; parenthetical addition mine)

Norenzayan attributes this phenomenon to unconscious concerns of being judged by a supernal observer. However, as will be discussed, concerns with the opinions of others, be they supernal beings or one's peers, play an important role in explaining the behavior of Americans today.

The *Oxford English Dictionary,* a frequent arbiter of final definitions, offers two alternatives. The first is "that which is in accordance with fact or reality"; the second, "a fact or belief that is *accepted as true.*" One can see that the latter leaves considerable room for difference of opinion, as *facts* are objective, whereas *beliefs* are not. Scientifically speaking, beliefs are neither necessarily true nor false; they are instead what individuals value as important and personally choose to accept. The first definition is objective and reproducible; the second is not, yet it has become increasingly commonplace.

Science ideally ignores beliefs and focuses exclusively on facts, which in turn must be confirmed by repeated observations.[8] But evidence suggests that critical standards of proof no longer are held in esteem by many,

---

8   It is common for post-modernist thinkers to apply observations in quantum mechanics, such as the Heisenberg uncertainty principle, to shore up their arguments that no facts exist per se, as we are all participatory observers. This is not the place to discuss the uncertainties of quantum theory, but suffice it to say it applies at a scale that man does not encounter in his daily life. At the scale of most human events, science is Newtonian and deterministic and not subject to substantial "uncertainty." Yet having said that, for complex systems, probabilities are also again important, but not in ways that apply to the arguments of most post-modernist social scientists.

including those in academia. Ignorance of facts is no longer is frowned upon; indeed, in some circles it appears to have become a virtue. In recent years, I have often been challenged in seminars by statements from attendees who claim that they are not interested in what science may have to say if it conflicts with how they feel about a matter. Belief has replaced facts as truth.

In a recent text, *The Death of Expertise* by Harvard professor Tom Nichols, the author quotes the scientist Isaac Asimov:

> There is a cult of ignorance in the United States, and there always has been one....nurtured by the false notion that democracy means that "my ignorance is just as good as your knowledge." (Nichols, 2017, p. 1)

Although, genuine expertise is laudable, it is currently questionable as to how many in the present-day academia merit the compliment. Too many "scholars" in academia, although formally educated, also currently base their opinions on politicized beliefs, rather than facts, and therefore differ little from those who they are quick to label as "ignorant."

The issue of what constitutes truth has profound implications for the future of our society. After all, how can groups be expected to establish discourse and to cooperate, if they cannot agree on what is true? As the philosopher Harry Frankfurt argues (Frankfurt, 2006):

> We live at a time when, strange to say, many quite cultivated individuals consider truth to be unworthy of any particular respect. It is well known, of course, that a cavalier attitude toward truth is more or less endemic within the ranks of publicists and politicians, breeds whose exemplars characteristically luxuriate in the production of bullshit; of lies, and of whatever other modes of fraudulence and fakery they are able to devise. That is old news and we are all accustomed to that. (Frankfurt, *Truth*, p. 17)

But Frankfurt reserves his greatest disdain for those academic "scholars" who, based on ideology, deny and even express contempt for the possibility of establishing "truth." These "shameless antagonists of common sense," as Frankfurt terms them, "refer to themselves as 'post-modernists,' and argue that truth has no exceptional privilege and that facts are of little importance compared to the perspectives that individuals bring to them" (Frankfurt, *Truth*, p. 18). Frankfurt views their position as both disingenuous and dangerous.

Truth has indeed been under siege for decades by post-modernist philosophers and by many psychotherapists who, attracted to post-modernist ideas, find it fashionable to espouse the notion that truth is "constructed" via intersubjective dynamics. The language adopted by post-modernist scholars can obfuscate and mislead, serving as an example of post-modern sophistry. Flexible truths and moral relativisms are too often touted as evidence of intellectual superiority and psychological enlightenment. Simple truths are condescendingly relegated to unenlightened "non-psychological" people. But like the child in Hans Christian Andersen's tale *The Emperor's New Clothes,* when post-modern concepts are critically probed, one discovers that "there is no there, there." Both psychoanalysis and the social sciences are replete with jargon that defies clarification. The language they adopt fosters paradox and ambiguity. In this sense, it is properly termed "mystical" (Katz, 1992), as it resists definition.[9] Admittedly, there may be a place for such approaches in the conduct of a symbolic insight-based psychotherapy, but it is not science. As Frankfurt suggests, "The natural and the social sciences, as well as the conduct of public affairs, surely cannot prosper except insofar as they carefully maintain the respect and concern (for the truth) (*Truth*, p. 16). Nor, in Frankfurt's view, is truth "optional" in pragmatic terms:

A society that is recklessly and persistently remiss in any of these

---

9   Prominent examples can be found in the work of the post-Freudians, including Winnicott, Bion, Lacan, etc. They include terms like "transitional objects," "liminal experiences," the absence of "memory and desire," and the "imaginal thirds," to name but a few. But ultimately, if it is to be therapeutic, psychological experience must return to everyday reality. The ego must interface with the real world, and if it is otherwise preoccupied with abstractions, neurosis will persist.

ways (concerning truth) is bound to decline or, at least, to render itself culturally inert. It will be certainly incapable of any substantial achievement, and even of any coherent and prudent ambitions. Civilizations have *never* gotten along healthily and *cannot* get along healthily, without large quantities of reliable *factual information*. They also cannot flourish if they are beset with troublesome infections of mistaken beliefs. To establish and to sustain an advanced culture, we need to avoid being debilitated either by error or by ignorance. (Frankfurt, *Truth*, p. 34; parenthetical addition mine)

The political philosopher Leo Strauss echoes these sentiments with respect to cultural truth. Arguing against the relativistic frame of historicism, Strauss states that "true freedom requires ends of a certain kind, and these ends have to be adopted in a certain manner. The ends must be anchored in ultimate values" (Strauss, 1953) p. 44).

But if truth cannot be determined, can agreement be achieved on what is good? As one might expect, the answer to that question is *no*.

Chapter 2: What Is Good?

Plato's notion of "the Good" informs the *unconstrained vision* (Bloom, 2016), but its more proximate roots may be found in the prophetic traditions of the Hebrew Bible. From a religious perspective, the ultimate "good" is God. As Jesus protested to his followers in Mark 10, "Why do you call me good? No one is good except God, alone." In today's secular society, what is "good" generally refers to how we treat our fellow-man, what some refer to as *ethical* good. The biblical prophets chided the Israelites to demonstrate concern for the vulnerable in society: the widow, the orphan, the poor, and the "alien who dwells among you."[10] Selfishness, greed, and seeking after fame, riches, and power were activities judged as morally bankrupt. New Testament scholar Bart Ehrman notes, "One of Jesus's characteristic teachings is that there will be a massive reversal of fortunes when the end time comes. Those who are rich and powerful now will be humbled then; those who are lowly and oppressed will be exalted" (Ehrman, 2012)p. 307).

But who is "vulnerable" is currently a topic of controversy in America. In a capitalist society, one is encouraged to accumulate private wealth. But the *unconstrained vision* holds that, in "truth," nothing belongs to individuals; instead, individual acquisitions are deemed public "gifts" to be shared selflessly with one's fellow man. In contrast, those who hold the *constrained vision* emphasize the rights of individuals to retain the fruits of their labors, although they are also encouraged to be charitable and to share a portion of their good fortune with those less fortunate. The Rabbis in antiquity discouraged giving more than 20% of one's earnings

---

10 Several of the letters of Paul in the New Testament refer to the collection that he was accumulating to give to the poor in Jerusalem. The latter are assumed to be the Jewish Christian Ebionites ("the poor"), leaders of the nascent Church. Caring for the underprivileged is a feature of all religions but was greatly accentuated in the early Church.

to charity, lest an overly generous donor find himself reliant on the charity of others.

Progressives who adopt the *unconstrained vision* view the federal government as the rightful benevolent overseer of the public welfare, whereas those who hold the *constrained vision* argue that government owns nothing of its own but is funded by taxes paid by its citizens, who should therefore determine its limits.

The mode of Progressivism that leans toward socialism is a religious argument reframed in secular terms. Instead of the notion that all things come from God, these Progressives have replaced God's authority with that of the federal government. Senator Elizabeth Warren, the current left-wing Progressive senator of Massachusetts—herself a multimillionaire—described her position this way:

> There is nobody in this country who got rich on his own—nobody. You built a factory out there? Good for you. But I want to be clear. You moved your goods to market on the roads the rest of us paid for. You hired workers the rest of us paid to educate. You were safe in your factory because of police-forces and fire-forces that the rest of us paid for. You didn't have to worry that marauding bands would come and seize everything at your factory—and hire someone to protect against this—because of the work the rest of us did. Now look, you built a factory and it turned into something terrific, or a great idea. God bless—keep a big hunk of it. But part of the underlying social contract is, you take a hunk of that and pay forward for the next kid who comes along. (Warren, CBS News. September 22, 2011)

Comparable socialist notions have repeatedly emerged on the American scene, but in the past they rarely gained traction. Traditionally, Americans have been suspect of ideologies that encroach upon their individual freedoms and hard-earned livelihood. In the 1950s, such views were considered threatening by many Americans. Then why do they persist as an alternative to capitalism in the imaginings of so many?

History has demonstrated that the *unconstrained vision* is often championed by an intellectual elite (Arendt, 1976). The leaders of ideological movements historically rarely emerge from the working classes. Instead they generally have been from privileged backgrounds and removed from the day-to-day concerns of the common man they claim to represent. Karl Marx, who co-authored *The Communist Manifesto*, was such an example. He was raised in a well-to-do family and according to his collaborator, Frederick Engels, he never held a steady job, was famously self-absorbed, and frankly derelict in providing for his own family (Mehring, 2003).

As Hannah Arendt argued, the common man can only be won over gradually to an ideology by sustained propaganda (Arendt, 1976). That approach had not been effective in America—until recently. But social media today can disseminate propaganda on a scale and pace previously unknown.[11] Left-leaning politicians, journalists, and entertainment and sports "stars" have all attempted to influence large segments of society through social media, and it has apparently been more effective than in times past.

Although the socialist message of the *unconstrained vision* holds appeal for some, for others it falls short. Conservative social commentator Charles Krauthammer suggests, "Progressive policies are naïve," as they ignore the known history of unsuccessful outcomes when they have been put into practice. The Marxist experiments of the twentieth century in Russia and China, and more recently in Cuba and Venezuela, have all been abject failures by any standard. Although democratic socialist policies in Europe have had a modicum of success, they have not inspired the entrepreneurial spirit that has characterized America's exceptionalism. Conservative social commentator David Horowitz notes (Horowitz, 2004):

> If socialism is not a viable system and capitalism is the only system that can produce wealth and freedom in a modern technological environment, what does this say about the revolutionary

---

11 Indeed, within Judaism, it has been argued that it is not permitted to make efforts to speed the coming of the Messianic age.

project? In the absence of a practical alternative, the revolutionary project is nihilism, the will to destroy without a concept of what to do next. (Horowitz, *Unholy*, p. 58)

Those who claim that Americans are greedy and unconcerned for others can provide little evidence to support their conclusions. America has had its share of corruption, but so has the rest of the world. Nor are Americans, as a whole, inured to the needs of the disadvantaged. On a per-dollar basis, the United States has objectively been the most charitable nation in the history of the world. Furthermore, like much of Western Europe and Canada, America has enacted its own "soft" socialist policies to ensure the survival of its poor, sick, and aged, including government-sponsored health care for the indigent (Medicaid), Social Security for the aged, and welfare entitlements for those who can justify receiving them.

Chapter 3: Utopia and the "Real" World

The tensions between utopian ideas and pragmatic concerns are not new. The idea of a perfected future "end time" figures prominently in all the Abrahamic monotheistic faiths. The prophetic visions vary, but in general it is imagined as a time of serenity. As it says in the prophecy of Isaiah 11, at the end of times, "The wolf will live with the lamb, the leopard will lie down with the goat, the calf and the lion and the yearling together; and a little child will lead them."

Eschatology, the scholarly study of the imagined end time, figures prominently in the approach to the intertestamental apocalyptic literature. The motifs in this ideologically driven literature are stereotypic. However, they describe times of great turbulence prior to the establishment of a lasting peace. They speak of a time when moral degeneracy has become so severe that prayers and repentance will be futile. Although always in the future, it is judged to be in many cases imminent. However, at the end of times, a moral elite will survive and be rewarded with divine revelation and salvation. Unfortunately, all others—by definition, anyone outside of the "in group"—will judged evil and will be condemned to God's wrath (Geza Vermes, 2012).

This ideology is driven by radical dualism in which "Good" and "Evil" are envisioned as ontological opposites. Radical dualism is seen in various forms. In the purer forms of monotheism, the opposing forces are all ultimately subject to the will of a Divine monad. In other forms, including Zoroastrianism and to a lesser extent Christianity, the elements of evil appear to be autonomous.

In Gnosticism, a Middle Platonic philosophy that was prevalent within Christianity in the second century, the universe was imagined to be inhabited by two deities. One was the supernal deity who ruled the spiritual realm and was the source of all that was good. The other, a demiurge, was a lesser divinity but unaware of the higher God. This lower deity was responsible for the creation of the material world, which was judged to be evil.

The entry of radical dual myth into monotheism is often attributed to the influence of the Persian Zoroastrian religion. Following the destruction of the first Jerusalem Temple in 586 BCE, many of the inhabitants of Judea were translocated to Babylon, which subsequently fell to the Medes and the Persians. When the Jews were allowed to return to their homeland in Judea to rebuild their Temple and function as part of the Persian empire, it is likely that aspects of radical dualism went with them (Stoyanov, 2000). But as Jung suggested, it is as likely that dualism represents the human psychological motif that tends to emerge in times of increased existential anxiety.

Christianity and the Apocalyptic Vision

Christianity began as an apocalyptic sect within the panoply of Second Temple Judaic sects (Cohen, 2014). As Albert Schweitzer noted in his magisterial *Search for the Historical Jesus*, early Christians eagerly awaited the end of times, when God would triumph in his final battle with Satan. This would usher in the Kingdom of God and final resurrection of the dead (Schweitzer, 1906). Schweitzer envisioned the historical Jesus as an apocalyptic seer who expected the imminent arrival of the Kingdom, and many current scholars of early Christianity concur (Ehrman, 2012).

Indeed, the features of apocalyptic vision can still be identified in Christianity, including notions of radical duality (God versus Satan), salvation limited to those who believe in Christ, and a final judgment at the end of times. For a variety of historical reasons, apocalyptic messianic

speculations were discouraged by the Rabbinic sages.[12] Excessive specu-
lation concerning what might happen in the future end time was frowned
upon if it led to ignoring the demands of present world and the existing
laws of society.

It is not far-fetched to describe the dueling *visions* in America today
as a secular expression of the ancient apocalyptic conflict between the
forces of "Good" and "Evil."[13] The commentator Charles Krauthammer
poignantly opined in 2002, "Conservatives think liberals are stupid. Liberals think conservatives are *evil*." He referred to this "a "fundamental
law" of modern American politics. He further argued that "Conservatives
are realists who favor policies that Liberals consider unduly cruel, even
evil" (Fox, 2017).

Psychologically, Freud attributed this antipathy to the "narcissism of
minor differences," often exhibited by closely related groups that differ
on what other might judge as minor points (S Freud, 1930), p. 331).[14]
This was certainly applicable to the enmity between the Jews and early Christians of the first century and also applies to what is transpiring

---

12 Messianism has been a repetitive trope in Judaism, each time followed by devas-
tating responses. The rise of the messianic movement, Christianity, ultimately led to
two millennia of persecution of Jews. The Jewish messianic Bar Kokhba rebellion of
132-135 CE led to a scorched earth response by Rome and the two-thousand-year exile
from their homeland. In the seventeenth century, the messianic emergence of Shabbtai
Tzvi resulted in widespread disillusionment of the Jews in the Diaspora. For these and
other reasons, the Rabbis were not enamored with messianic concepts, although they are
a staple of Orthodox theology.

13 It is uncertain where this idea originated, but it first appears in Judaism after the Babylonian
exile. It is a core element of Persian Zoroastrianism and may have entered the consciousness of
Judaism from there.

14 The other apocalyptic sect of Judaism in the first century CE was the group that
authored the Dead Sea Scrolls. Their writings reveal a radical duality of thought and
a desire to rid Judea of the other sects, especially those who administered the Temple.
These sects differed in minor ways but the psychological effects were huge. After the
destruction of the Temple, the only sects to survive were the Pharisees who gave rise to
what we currently refer to as Rabbinic Judaism and the early Christians. These would
eventually part ways in mutual antipathy.

between Conservatives and Progressive Americans today. As Americans, both groups share more in common than they will admit.

American Religion

The Yale polymath David Gelernter argues in *Americanism* (Gerlernter, 2007) that:

America is no secular republic; it's a biblical republic. Americanism is not a civic religion; it's a biblical religion.... America is one of the most beautiful religious concepts mankind has ever known. It's sublimely humane, built on strong evidence of humanity's ability to make life better. (Gelernter, *Americanism*, p. 1)

Since its Puritan beginnings in New England, America has been informed by the Judeo-Christian ethic. Both the *constrained* and *unconstrained visions* can locate their core values within the Judeo-Christian tradition, although they emphasize different ideas as to what constitutes the highest "Good" in society. To better appreciate this, one must consider the essential differences between Judaism and Christianity.

Traditionally, Jews saw themselves as a group set apart by God to live a life of Priestly purity, as defined by the commandments set out in scripture and Rabbinic law. Traditional Jews were preoccupied with rituals affecting all aspects of their daily life, how they ate, when they prayed, how they dressed, etc. They understood themselves as "chosen" to spread the idea of monotheism to the pagan "nations." Today, most non-Orthodox Jews in post-Enlightenment America profess secular values and have abandoned most of the "legal" barriers that set them apart from their non-Jewish neighbors.

Christianity is a syncretistic merger of the *constrained vision* of Jewish particularism and the *unconstrained vision* of Hellenistic universalism. After 323 BCE, Judea was part of Alexander's Hellenistic empire. In 63 BCE, it passed peacefully into Roman rule, but the essential elements of Hellenism were well entrenched. The Hebrew Bible had been translated into Greek, and Jews in Judea likely were to some extent bilingual, speaking Aramaic amongst themselves and Greek with foreigners. Whereas it is widely assumed that Jesus spoke Aramaic, the New Testament was entirely written in Greek.

Many Jews lived in the Greek-speaking Diaspora. In addition, evidence suggests that many urban pagans were enamored with Judaism and attended the synagogues. They were termed God-fearers, but few submitted to conversion. Following Jesus' crucifixion, his followers attempted to convince their fellow Jews of his messiahship, but largely without success. However, many pagans were convinced but few were willing to convert to Judaism with its stringent dietary requirement, sexual prohibitions, and requirement for male circumcision, a painful procedure for an adult.

By Paul's insistence that pagan converts need not—and moreover must not—adopt Judaism, Christianity was able to attract many pagan converts. These new Christians were subject to following retained the Hebrew Bible's Ten Commandments but ignored the remaining laws of Judaism in the first century. As pagans from the Hellenized world, their ties to Judaism's strict form of monotheism and Jewish ethnicity were weak. Over time, the two groups developed a bitter antipathy. It is noteworthy that other moral philosophies were also established in the Roman Empire at the time of the emergence of Christianity and Rabbinic Judaism, and these undoubtedly influenced the *ethos* of both religions. As Wayne Meeks (1993) notes: (Meeks, 1993)

> The superimposition of Roman power on the towns of Italy and the East, the linkages of local aristocracies with the Roman leaders, the emigration of peoples in an age of freer and safer travel and commerce—all these factors and more changed the face of urban culture. Nevertheless, for the elites who articulated the language of moral obligation, the city remained the primary framework of reference. (p. 13)

This was true for the Jews of the Diaspora who retained their focus on particularism, but likely even more so for the early Christian pagan converts.

Although America, as Gelernter (2007) notes, is at its core a religious nation, the traditional practices of Christianity and Judaism are not observed in most homes today. Religion in America has taken on what the social critic Harold Bloom sees as a unique type of secular transformation that would not be easily recognized in other countries (Bloom 1993).

Most Americans continue to self-describe as Christians. According to a Pew poll in 2015 (Newport, 2015):

> On the eve of Christmas 2015, a review of over 174,000 interviews conducted in 2015 shows that three-quarters of American adults identify with a Christian religion.... About 5% of Americans identify with a non-Christian religion, while 20% have no formal religious identification, which is up five percentage points since 2008.

How does religious observance track with those who adopt the constrained and unconstrained visions? Americans in the Midwest and South, which includes the agricultural heartland and fewer ethnic minorities and immigrants, tend to vote along Conservative lines and support the *constrained vision*. These areas are home to the Christian evangelical "Bible Belt," and religion continues to play a critical role in their beliefs and practices.

Progressives are concentrated in the large urban areas of America, and especially on its coasts. These urban areas are home to large numbers of academic scholars, minorities, new immigrants, and those in the entertainment and technology industries. As one might predict, Progressives in urban America are less engaged in religious practices. However, they purport to be more concerned about issues of social justice than their Conservative counterparts.[15] Indeed, many Progressives eschew all traditional religion, which they view as an impediment to social progress. As few are conversant with the history of religion, they will fail to recognize that their beliefs are rooted, not in secular thought, but in traditional religion.

---

15 The Church was split into Roman Catholic and Eastern Orthodox sects in 1054. The reference to "orthodoxy" reflects the accepted dogma of the Church, not any particular branch.

In his *Moral Politics,* the cognitive psychologist George Lakoff contrasts what he describes as *Strict Parent* versus *Nurturant Parent,* which parallel the differences between Conservative and Progressive ideologies, respectively. Lakoff (2016) writes:(Lakoff, 2016)

> In *Strict Parent* Christianity, God is a moral authority and the role of human beings is to obey his strict commandments. The way you learn to obey is by being punished for not obeying and by developing the self-discipline to obey through strict denial. In *Nurturant Parent* Christianity, God is a nurturer and the proper relationship to God is to accept his nurturance (Grace) and follow Christ's example of how to act nurturantly toward others. There are no strict rules; rather one must develop empathy and learn to act compassionately for the benefit of others, whatever they might require.

Although there is some merit in Lakoff's characterization of these positions as what is driving the poles of America's political conflicts, he fails to point out that it is possible to be Conservative or Progressive and value *both* positions.

Traditional Judaism, too often mischaracterized as a *Strict Parent* religion by those insufficiently conversant with its tenets, is in fact the source of both positions. For example, the "social justice" agenda of the Progressive left was formulated for the first time in recorded history within the Hebrew Bible, and it is fundamental to traditional Jewish morality.[16] The ancient Israelites are repeatedly warned that, "The alien who dwells among you shall be to you as one born among you, and thou shalt love him as thyself; for you also were aliens in the land of Egypt: I am the LORD your God." But it adds that there must be one standard of justice for all: "The same law applies both to the native-born and to the foreigner residing among you." These are the most repeated verses in the Hebrew Bible.

---

16 The Reform and Conservative movements in American Judaism today have increasingly adopted the tenets of the "Nurturing Parent" and have largely dismissed the legal tenets of traditional Judaism. Their failure to value the potential character-building effects of legal observance has resulted in a distortion of Jewish values, and many of these religionists are now squarely positioned in the domain of left-wing Progressivism.

Therefore, the political choice is not whether one is compassionate versus preoccupied with enforcing punishments; the message is that they are both required. Lakoff's analysis of Christian morality fails to recognize that the choice is not between being a strict or nurturing parent; indeed, the truly good parent must find the balance between these extremes.

Founding a Christian Nation

The treatises of John Locke, John Stuart Mill, and other famed British philosophers informed the Founding Fathers' ideas on liberty and human rights. The leading minds of the British Enlightenment, whatever their personal degree of religiosity, were well versed in the Holy Scriptures (Gerlernter, 2007; Huntington, 2005). The Founding Fathers conceived of America as a nation that favored religious freedoms, but they were also determined to reject the infringements of state-sponsored religion. Their chief concern was not that religion would undermine the daily life of its citizens, as the American colonists were, on the whole, already God-fearing. Rather, it was that a state religion might achieve hegemony over the polity, as it had England and the European mainland. What some Progressive opponents of religion claim today to be the legal "separation of Church and State" is not what the Founding Fathers intended or could possibly have imagined when they drafted the Establishment and Free Exercise Clauses of the First Amendment as part of the Bill of Rights.

The Founders were pragmatists; they worked to achieve a compromise between the *constrained* and *unconstrained visions* for the new nation. Some, like Thomas Jefferson, were Deists (Ellis, 2015).[17] But they virtually all agreed on the importance of Christian morality for the new nation. They were certainly attuned to the Old Testament prophet Samuel, who warned about the excesses and abuses of kings:

He will appoint for himself commanders of thousands and of fifties, and

---

17 Deists like Jefferson believed that the world had been created by God but did not think that he continued to intervene in the daily lives of men. Jefferson had written his own Gospels that were limited to the sayings of Jesus.

some to do his plowing and to reap his harvest and to make his weapons of war and equipment for his chariots. He will take your daughters as perfumers and cooks. He will take the best of your fields and your vineyards and your olive groves and give them to his servants....

The Founders recognized that power, when concentrated in the hands of a few, was likely to corrupt and lead to tyranny. America had just fought a war to rid itself of a tyrannical English king, and George Washington refused the offer of a crown and instead accepted the title of President.

But the Founders were not egalitarians. Alexander Hamilton recognized the inequalities between men, and, like Plato, he was partial to the idea of an intellectual elite ruling the new nation. In the *Federalist Papers,* he argued that the new nation would best be structured as a republic rather than as a democracy. As Hamilton suggested in a speech in 1788 urging ratification of the new Constitution:

It has been observed that a pure democracy if it were practicable would be the most perfect government. Experience has proved that no position is more false than this. The ancient democracies in which the people themselves deliberated never possessed one good feature of government. Their very character was tyranny; their figure deformity. (Hamilton, address to New York delegation, June 21, 1788)

To curb the accumulation of power, the Founders imposed a system of checks and balances on the new government, and a novel method of electing a president through an Electoral College that limited the influence of the most populous states.[18] The new system of government relied on the *constrained vision* in its acceptance of human imperfection. The American experiment has been successful for more than two centuries. But its success would not be duplicated in France a decade later, for reasons at-

---

18 The election of a president who has lost the popular vote has occurred five times. These include John Quincy Adams in 1824, Rutherford Hayes in 1876, Benjamin Harrison in 1888, George W. Bush in 2000, and Donald Trump in 2016. Those Democrats who complain that the most recent election results are unfair appear not to recognize how the Electoral College system works and why it was instituted—to avoid imbalanced representation by populous individual states.

tributable to the different mythic visions that guided their experiments.

French Revolution

The French and American Revolutions demonstrate how the *unconstrained* and *constrained* visions, respectively, work in practice. The American Revolution began in 1776, the French revolt in 1789. Whereas both were rooted in Enlightenment philosophies, the French experiment was primarily the expression of the *unconstrained vision*, conceived based on Rousseau's idealized concept of "liberty, equality, fraternity," as a democracy that insisted upon man's perfectibility.

The French revolt was a secular enterprise. The Catholic Church had been intertwined with the power structures of the French aristocracy since the eighth, and clerics were highly unpopular with the peasantry (Schama, 1990). The French Revolution began with attacks on the corruption of the Catholic Church and on its ill-gained wealth. The Revolution suppressed French churches, nationalized church property, exiled 30,000 priests, violently removed its Catholic monarchy, and killed hundreds more (Holmes, 2016).

The idealism of the Revolution quickly devolved into the Reign of Terror. As the historian Kim Holmes suggests (Holmes, 2016):

> The Jacobins who followed Robespierre in establishing the *Reign of Terror* shared…a philosophy of "natural republicanism"; they believed that individuals who transgressed the laws of nature must be executed without judicial formalities. Anyone who stood against the republic stood against the people who were by right of their natural *goodness* above reproach. An enemy of the people became an enemy of humanity and thus guilty of treason. (Holmes, *Closing*, pp. 217-18)

It is estimated that the French Reign of Terror resulted in as many as 40,000 deaths and required the dictatorship of Napoleon to restore order.

By contrast, the earlier American Revolution was the product of a mercantile and agrarian society guided primarily by the *constrained vision.* The American colonists were not peasants, and they demanded being treated as loyal and proper English citizens. The Revolution was carried out by colonists who resented being treated as "second class" citizens, and the notion of "no taxation without representation," a driving popular cry amongst the American colonists, was inconceivable for a French peasantry that had never tasted any degree of equality with the nobility.

Envy and Ressentiment

The radical French experiment was motivated by envy and long-standing resentment. The peasantry hated its ruling class, as it had no hope of ever sharing in its wealth or comforts. Once in power, they called for the redistribution of wealth—an idea that has reemerged on the American political left. Envy is a strong psychological motivating factor and can propel violent actions. But the politics of envy cannot be sustained without eventually turning inward and devouring itself. Movements based in envy begin with acts of destruction and then devolve into anarchy or tyranny, precisely because they lack the necessary structural framework to ensure societal stability.

As Phillip Rieff suggests, Freud was aware of the role of envy in political revolts, and recognized it as a psychological force fueling instability (Rieff, 1979). He writes:

> By psychologizing social revolt and coercion Freud weights his scale against impulse and in favor of law. Society is repressive; rebellion is not justified. For the freedom that humans seek is still the freedom to be master. The "conscious impulses" of rebellion have their unconscious sources in envy. (Rieff, *Mind,* p. 227)

The French Revolution was the template for subsequent envy-based revolutions. But what should have been a one-time failed lesson in history would be repeated in Russia in 1917, and as Italian Fascism and German National Socialism in the mid-twentieth century. All called for a new

47

egalitarian society and for the perfectibility of man; all resulted in large numbers of deaths; and all ultimately failed.

Yet left-wing Progressives will rarely admit that these revolts were ill-conceived. Instead, they offer rationalizations for why they in fact did *not* fail. As a member of the socialist Green Party recently concluded, "There simply is no reason to examine the validity of socialism as a model. It is not socialism that was defeated in Eastern Europe and in the Soviet Union, because these systems were never socialist" (Horowitz, 2004) p. 58).

Two hundred years after the French debacle, the radical reformer Saul Alinsky—the acknowledged political mentor of both Hillary Clinton and Barack Obama—would argue, like the Jacobins, that revolutions must be extreme in their willingness to destroy what came before so that something "new" can emerge (Alinsky, 1971). It is a compelling argument in the abstract, but history does not support its conclusion.

Chapter 4: Morality in America

The *Oxford English Dictionary* defines morality as the "principles concerning the distinction between right and wrong or good and bad behavior." But this definition does little to clarify the distinction. In his magisterial text *After Virtue*, the philosopher Alasdair MacIntyre critically examines what is meant by "morality."(Mac Intyre, 2007) He concludes that post-Enlightenment ideas of secular individuality have hopelessly eroded the meaning of morality by loosing it from the societal and religious principles that they must remain embedded in, if they are to provide any consensual meaning. Much as there was no concept of "religion" until the emergence of secularism, there was no isolated idea of "morality." Subsequent post-Enlightenment philosophical efforts to define morality rationally as imperative, utilitarian, pragmatic, or based on "societal good" do not bear up to a rigorous philosophical analysis. The result has been an "emotivist" definition that frees morality from anything more than what "feels" best to the individual, which is an obvious invitation to undermining the fabric of a society. As MacIntyre notes:

The problems of modern moral theory emerge clearly as the product of the failure of the Enlightenment Project. On the one hand the individual moral agent, freed from hierarchy and teleology, conceives of himself and is conceived of by moral philosophers as sovereign in his moral authority. On the other hand, the inherited, if partially transformed rules of morality have to be found some new status, deprived as they have been of their older teleological character and their even more ancient categorical character as expressions of an ultimately divine law.

Simply put, the idea of an individualistic morality divorced from its theological roots is a non-sequitur. Yet it is exactly what is currently being argued for by Progressives in America. Terms like virtue and morality cannot be extricated from their traditional sources because modern secular society cannot define them without interminable argument and conflict.

Since the 1960s in America, antagonistic views of what is "moral" have rapidly increased based on societal changes that have influenced perspectives on what is good and bad, most prominently the civil rights movement, feminism, and social media. The consequences of these changes have increased divisiveness; and their pitfalls are rarely openly discussed or criticized because when morality is "emotive," there is no basis for rational argument. Nevertheless, the roots of moral emotivism remain schizophrenically embedded in the Judeo-Christian ethic.

Overtly bigoted Jim Crow Southern expressions of racism and the more covert or "polite" forms of racism typically seen in the North are rarely seen in today's America. But despite obvious gains in civil rights, a rabid form of identity politics has emerged and threatens to strain race relations and their natural evolution. Feminism has transformed women's participation in the workplace, and contraception and abortion have freed women from the biological consequences of their sexual activity. But it has contributed to the undermining of domestic stability, with increased divorce rates and questionably positive changes in styles of child-rearing.

These changes have raised new challenges to societal stability and traditional notions of objective truth. For example, new ideas concerning gender currently challenge long-standing *scientific conclusions* about sexual difference. Biology, the primary scientific determinant of gender, has been dismissed by those Progressives who prefer to *believe* that gender is a matter of choice, or like their post-modernist notions of truth, "constructed" by caretakers who had been inculcated by a patriarchal society that is currently irrelevant. But this opinion runs counter to facts. The politicization of science has resulted in erroneous and potentially dangerous ideas being promulgated by institutions that should remain unaligned and unaffected by political positions.

Consider an official statement in 2017 by the American Academy of Pediatrics (Pediatrics, 2017), an organization widely thought to be an evidenced-based *scientific* organization, which warned parents that children as young as three years of age should be encouraged to question their gender identity:

> The American Academy of Pediatrics stands in support of trans-gender children and adults, and condemns attempts to stigmatize or marginalize them. We believe transgender individuals are not a "disruption." They are members of our families, our communities, and our work force.

This may appeal to the feelings of some, but what is the scientific basis for such ideas? Do Progressive concerns about "stigma" justify dismissing scientific facts? Can a naïve and suggestible three-year-old be expected to know his or her "gender"? There is no objective evidence to support that notion, and pre-pubertal imaginings tend to be fluid in young minds on many issues, including gender. Is a three-year-old boy who enjoys playing with dolls destined to want to be a woman when he grows older? Or the young girl tomboy meant to be a man? Few rational adults would conclude that. Yet a three-year-old boy or girl would likely know their gender based on the biological differences in their anatomy.

Whereas one might leniently be inclined to forgive politicians and even social "scientists" for promoting doubt and ambiguity about "facts," there is no excuse for such positions being espoused by medical "scientists." But this is the result of the widespread politicization of American institutions, and an example of the herd mentality or what has been termed "groupthink" amongst Progressive-leaning institutions that until recently had been immune to the effects of political propaganda.

Consider an article that appeared in the *Daily Wire* quoting Paul McHugh, the former chief of psychiatry at Johns Hopkins, a prestigious medical institution (Prestigiacomo, 2016):

> Former Chief of Psychiatry at Johns Hopkins Hospital and Distinguished Service Professor of Psychiatry at Johns Hopkins University Dr. Paul R. McHugh blasted the Left's transgender movement, saying that those who enable the mental illness of transgenderism are "col-

laborating with madness."

Dr. McHugh has had a long and distinguished career. He would certainly qualify by Nichols's standards as someone with "expertise." But his statement was widely ridiculed by Progressives and the mainstream press as "politically incorrect." But "political correctness" has no place in the practice of evidence-based medical psychiatry. Politicized science is dangerous; one need only look to the "scientific" experiments conducted by Nazi doctors (Lifton, 2000) or those that took place in Communist Russia under Stalin.

At least some disinterested psychotherapists who have treated transsexual patients will attest that these individuals present a host of psychological issues that are not directly related to their "gender choice." Furthermore, there are serious consequences to interventions aimed at changing one's biological sex. The effects of surgeries that alter secondary sexual characteristics can have severe deleterious effects. A study from Germany reported the following surgical complications (Rossi Neto, Hintz, Krege, Rübben, & vom Dorp):

> Progressive obstructive voiding disorder due to meatal stenosis was the main complication observed in 40% of the patients, feasibly corrected during the second setting. Stricture recurrence was found in 15%. Stricture of vaginal introitus was observed in 15% of the cases followed by 12% and 8% of vaginal stenosis and loss of vaginal depth, respectively. Rectal injury was seen in 3% and minor wound healing disorders in 33% of the subjects.

Another study from Sweden reported not only surgical complications but a significant risk of suicide following these procedures (Dhejne et al., 2011):

> The overall mortality for sex-reassigned persons was higher during follow-up (2.8; 95% CI 1.8–4.3) than for controls of the same birth sex, particularly death from suicide (19.1; 95% CI 5.8–62.9). Sex-reassigned persons also had an increased risk for suicide attempts (4.9; 95% CI 2.9–8.5) and psychiatric inpatient care (2.8; 95% CI 2.0–3.9).

Comparisons with controls matched on reassigned sex yielded similar results. Female-to-males, but not male-to-females, had a higher risk for criminal convictions than their respective birth sex controls.

The guiding principle of medical practice since Hippocrates has been *"primum non nocere,"* or "first, do no harm." A physician's political or moral beliefs should not determine whether an elective medical procedure is conducted, no matter how psychologically distressed a patient may be. Obviously, there are physicians who feel differently about the matter. To what extent this may represent progress is open to question, but it is certainly not science.

To *believe* that one is a member of the opposite sex is what psychiatrists until recently would have agreed was "delusional" thinking. To insist, as some Progressive gender egalitarians do, that anyone can simply declare their preferred gender and then expect, and more critically insist, that others also accept this as truth, is indicative of a society that has undergone a substantial shift in morality. The argument that acknowledging the truth about biologically determined gender is *cruel* to transsexuals has no agreed-upon basis; it is not a psychological truth, but is a perspective, and primarily a political statement. Truth is not stigmatizing when it is properly understood, communicated compassionately, and ultimately accepted. Facts until recently have been the basis of "reality testing." When psychologists, physicians, and the lay public deny reality, they collude with psychosis.

Biological science and medicine have been carefully developed over centuries based on the empirical study of anatomical and physiological *facts*, not opinions. The suggestion that gender has nothing to do with anatomy is not what we should be hearing from medical scientists in the twenty-first century. Scientists are supposed to divest themselves of bias, not embrace it. Progressivism, which traditionally had championed a scientific disposition, should not allow itself to be hijacked by "magical thinking."

Homosexuality was, and is still, condemned within many traditional societies because it does not lead to the procreation of the species. In the heyday of psychoanalysis, which lasted through the 1960s, "enlightened" psychiatrists viewed homosexuality as an intractable neurosis with narcissistic underpinnings. Today, most Americans accept homosexuality as a way of life and as genetically determined, although the science underlying the latter claim is at best weak. Consider the results of a study reported by the psychologist Robert Spitzer (Spitzer, 2003).Spitzer interviewed more than 200 people, most of whom claimed that, through reparative therapy counseling, their desires for same-sex partners either diminished significantly or they changed over to heterosexual orientation. Although still a proponent of homosexual activism, Spitzer has been attacked unmercifully by former admirers for this breach of the ideology that people are "born gay and can't change." Immutability is a central tenet of demands for "gay rights" and "gay marriage." Because no single study can be regarded as definitive, more research on people who have overcome homosexuality needs to be done. But a considerable body of previous literature about change from homosexuality to heterosexuality has been compiled, and the sheer number of exceptions to the "born gay" theory should be a warning to researchers and media to proceed with caution before declaring that science has "proved" that homosexuality is innately determined.

Whereas many Americans applaud society's acceptance of homosexuality as progress, others harbor concerns that problems that had in the past been strongly associated with the "gay" lifestyle, including promiscuity, illicit drug use, and sexually transmitted diseases, are now largely unaddressed. But other concerns pertain to whether America is going to strive toward being an integrated society or whether America will allow itself to fragment based on gender, race, religion, etc.

A recent controversy concerned the demand of homosexual veterans to march as a separate group (the *Out Vets*) in the annual St. Patrick's Day parade in South Boston. When the event organizers requested that the Out Vets march with their fellow non-homosexual veterans as a sign of veteran solidarity, they adamantly refused. The *Out Vets*, supported by the liberal mayor of Boston and like-minded Progressive city legislators, were intent on making a statement about their homosexual identity, which was apparently more important to them than their identity as American veterans. In addition, St. Patrick's Day, originally an Irish Catholic observance, has no basis in celebrations of homosexuality, but that too was ignored. Progressive Americans are splitting themselves into ever smaller factions, each with its own political agenda. But as Lincoln warned prior to the advent of the Civil War, "A house divided cannot stand." America, fragmented into innumerable factions, each with its own claims to legitimacy, faces a similar challenge today.

The Fiction of Rampant Racism in America

Despite tangible and steady advances in civil rights since the 1960s, accusations of racism have increased in America. The hope that the first black American president might actively promote racial harmony was not fulfilled. A CNN poll in 2016 found that "overall, 54% of Americans say relations between blacks and whites have gotten worse since Obama became president, including 57% of whites and 40% of blacks" (Agiesta, 2016).

Strident Progressive voices and violent elements within the black community insist that sufficient progress has not been made in civil rights and that "black lives matter," in their opinion, more than *all* lives do. People of color on college campuses have made exceptional demands with respect to admissions, accommodations, grading, and curricula, and too often these have been met by Progressive administrators.

In extraordinary displays of self-hatred, some vocal Progressive whites have denounced not only racial bigotry, but the very *legitimacy* of being white. As Dinesh D'Souza notes in his 1991 text *Illiberal Education*, one liberal professor noted that he didn't mind being called a "honkey" by blacks because, he said, "whites deserve it" (D'Souza, 1991). Some Progressive academics have suggested that whiteness is a "pathology." In one case, a *white* male college professor issued a statement that he was "dreaming of a white genocide for Christmas." Despite the outrageous nature of such statements, they have been sanctioned by Progressive "scholars" on college campuses. Consider this response from the University of Wisconsin administration:

A spokesman for the University of Wisconsin-Madison has shrugged off concerns over one of its students selling hoodies bearing the phrase "All White People Are Racist" in capital letters: "In this case, the individuals involved are exercising their rights to free speech and engaging in a private activity unrelated to their status as students," campus spokesman John Lucas said in an email to *The College Fix*. (October 26, 2016)

If such speech was tolerated by all, this might be an acceptable response. But were a white student to criticize black students in this manner, it is virtually certain that it would be considered "hate speech" and grounds for expulsion.

"Hands Up! Don't Shoot"

A dangerous disregard for law is occurring daily in America's urban neighborhoods. Thousands of people have died over the last ten years in the city of Chicago, the majority as the result of "black on black" crime.

More than 750 people have been murdered in Chicago in 2016, the police said, a 58 percent increase over last year and the highest total since 1997. There have been more than 3,500 shootings in the city this year. Over Christmas weekend, at least 60 people were shot, 11 fatally, according to the Chicago Tribune. (*New York Times*, Dec 28, 2016)

These are facts. These numbers exceed the Americans killed in recent wars in the Middle East and are *far* greater than the number of blacks killed in the line of duty by white policeman (McDonald, 2016). Yet Progressive mayors, governors, the mainstream press, and former President Obama have consistently ignored these statistics, presumably because they do not conform with the Progressive narrative that only whites persecute blacks.

Riots erupted in Ferguson, Missouri, after Michael Brown, a black man, was killed by a white policeman. The policeman claimed self-defense, whereas others claimed that the black man had his hands up in the air and was asking not to be shot. Progressives and President Obama, without examining the facts, opted to support the narrative of "victimization." But when the *evidence* was examined by a grand jury, the "hands up, don't shoot" story was rejected as false based on the eyewitness testimony by black citizens who testified under oath that Brown had indeed attacked and threatened the officer. But the facts did little to reverse the false claims that the victim had been unjustly "murdered." The violent riots continued, and no formal admission of having been incorrect was offered to the nation by its leaders.

The Attack on Free Speech

Freedom of speech, guaranteed by the First Amendment to the Constitution, has been curtailed by an insidious culture of *political correctness* that limits speech based on the imaginings of an influential minority that speech *might* harm others. Certainly, words *can* be harmful when they are overtly abusive. But a problem arises when the final arbiters of speech are either inordinately hypersensitive or politically motivated to censor free speech with the purpose of creating a new social order.

Some examples of politically correct speech appear, at face value, too absurd to be considered seriously by most rational adults, yet that has not stopped them from becoming policy on some university campuses and workplaces. Accusations of "bigotry" and "racism" are routinely put forward to malign the reputations of people who express opposing opinions that were once considered "benign" or even humorous. Those who are accused may not be allowed to defend themselves or informed as to who brought the accusations.

There is an ancient story known to scholars of early Christianity about Pliny the Younger, who was a governor in a Roman province who asked the Emperor Trajan how to deal with accusations made against Christians by their pagan neighbors. Trajan responded that no Christian should be punished based on anonymous claims (Meeks, 1993). It seems that 2000 years ago, it was clear to a pagan Roman Emperor that anonymous accusations were potentially tainted and could not be used to infer guilt. But that is no longer generally true in America.

Violent protests have occurred on college campuses when Conservative speakers invited to lecture have dared to express views that differ with Progressive morals. A list of accomplished Conservative and Libertarian scholars, many of whom are acknowledged experts in their fields, have been heckled off college campuses with angry epithets and physical threats. William Bennett, a former Secretary of Health, Education, and Welfare, stated in a July 28, 2016, television interview that he and other Conservative intellectuals had not been invited to speak on Ivy League college campuses for decades. The political scientist Alan Bloom bemoaned this as nothing short of the "closing of the American mind" (Bloom, 2012):

Every educational system has a moral goal that it tries to attain and that informs its curriculum. It wants to produce a certain kind of human being. . . . In some nations, the goal was the pious person, in others the warlike, in others the industrious. Always important is the political regime, which needs citizens who are in accord with its fundamental principle. Aristocracies want gentlemen, oligarchies men who respect and pursue money, and democracies lovers of equality. Democratic education, whether it admits it or not, wants and needs to produce men and women who have the tastes, knowledge, and character supportive of a democratic regime. (Bloom, *Closing*, p. 26) Unfortunately, what Bloom applauds is no longer the case on too many college campuses in America today.

Sexual Abuse by Men

In a recent case at Columbia University, one repeated across American campuses, young male students accused of "rape" were expelled without recourse against what ultimately were proved to be false allegations of misconduct.

Even though Columbia found him not responsible for what had been alleged [rape], his suit claims the school was complicit in [his accuser's] long-running effort to destroy his reputation and declined to intervene because he is male. Some people believe the claim is absurd. Others say it's the wake-up call higher education needs to start protecting *all* students. (*Newsweek,* December 18, 2015)

The once liberal notion that one must be considered "innocent until proven guilty" no longer applies on some Progressive college campuses and workplaces. This is a radical change in traditional American values and legal standards. The recent "Me Too" movement that has exposed sexual indiscretions by a seemingly ever-growing list of men in Hollywood, the press, and politics, and it may indeed represent genuine progress if it helps to correct sexual misconduct at the workplace. But there have also always been *false* claims made by women against innocent men. The biblical narrative in Genesis describes Joseph as wrongly accused by the spurned wife of his Egyptian overlord, and unjustly punished.

If justice is to be preserved, misconduct must be established in each case by facts, not by innuendo. Genuine progress should not devolve into a "reign of terror," with male heads rolling indiscriminately. Concerning the sexual misconduct charges brought against the actor Jeremy Piven, a recent commentary in the *Chicago Tribune* notes (O'Neill, 2017):

After describing the accusations against him as "absolutely false," Iven laments the fact that "allegations are being printed as facts" and "lives are being put in jeopardy without a hearing, due process or evidence." He wonders what happened to "the benefit of the doubt." To "tear each other down and destroy careers based on mere allegations is not productive at all," he says.

News and Views

The last twenty-five years have seen the explosive impact of the Internet and social media on societal values. New sources of news reporting have encroached on traditional print and televised media. It is currently possible for virtually anyone to share observations and opinions on all manner of topics via social media. Unfortunately, few of these amateur information providers have been trained as journalists.

Partisan journalism is not new to America. Indeed, only since the twentieth century have journalists been formally educated to act as objective unbiased reporters of news and to verify their sources as legitimate. Biased "yellow journalism" was decried, and some media outlets (e.g., the *New York Times* and *Washington Post*) acquired a reputation for high-quality investigative news reporting. But this was before digital media shortened the news cycle from several days to several minutes. Mainstream newspapers, including the *New York Times* and *Washington Post,* and television stations (ABC, NBC, CBS) have been purchased by large Progressive-leaning corporate conglomerates.

The primacy of belief over fact has created a culture of fallacious "facts." The mainstream press today unapologetically promotes the Progressive agenda to an extent not seen in recent times. The 2016 U.S. Presidential campaign and its aftermath have been so plagued by faulty and biased journalism that it is no longer possible for readers or viewers to know when, or if, they are being told "the truth." Few retractions or apologies are offered when such news stories are demonstrated to be inaccurate (Kurtz, 2018).

Whatever one may feel about the current president, there can be little doubt that there has been an unprecedented, unrelenting, and concerted effort to denigrate and resist virtually every action of President Trump and his administration by the mainstream press. This is not polemic; it is a *fact* supported by a recent Pew Poll that demonstrated that only 5% of the stories in the mainstream media have touted the accomplishments of the Trump presidency. This number is far lower than that of any other U.S. president in recent history. The Trump administration's impact has been positive, with unquestionable achievements in a variety of areas, most notably the economy, which has shown a steep recovery since Trump's election (Bedard, 2017).

The most recent contribution to this biased attack has been a poll of 128 political scientists who, one year into Trump's administration, have voted him the "worst president in U.S. history." The same poll rated Barack Obama as one of the ten greatest American presidents (Kwong, 2018). Certainly, most unbiased scientists would conclude that it is premature to make conclusions concerning a presidency one year into a four-year term, not to mention what many might consider remarkably positive effects that have transpired in the American economy during Trump's time in office. As for the rating of Mr. Obama, one political pundit remarked, "Exactly what did he accomplish in eight years?" But this is not to debate the relative merits of these two presidencies; it is merely further support for claims of bias in the Progressive media and its supporters.

Chapter 5: A Neurotic Society

The degree of polarization in America suggests an underlying psychological cause. The psychology of groups is complex but, in many respects, paradoxically simpler than that of individuals. People in groups are more sensitive to influence and tend to oversimplify complex issues. Social psychologists have long recognized that societies can periodically assume the features of neurosis and even frank madness. Examples of mass hysteria have occurred repeatedly in history (e.g., the witch craze that persisted for centuries with the death of thousands, mostly women, and culminating in the New England Salem trials). Germany was infected by a collective group madness in the mid-twentieth century, in which an educated, civilized people were driven to extreme depravity. In these instances, the strong beliefs held by a small group in power succeeded in infecting an entire nation with propaganda and overwhelmed truth and the standards of civilized morality.

At their root, neuroses are caused by lies that we tell ourselves and others. The traditional approach to the treatment of neuroses is to restore well-being by encouraging patients to confront self-deceptions, take responsibility for them, and work at correcting them. At best, this is a difficult undertaking. But to achieve this, the patient and therapist must first be able to agree on what constitutes truth, and patients must have the capacity to accept responsibility for their actions. One need only recall the biblical story of the fall in the Garden of Eden to recognize how ancient the problem is. After disobeying God's command not to eat from the Tree of Knowledge, Adam and Eve both deny responsibility for their actions, and instead blame each other and the serpent, as well, for what has transpired.[19]

---

19 The "Fall" is generally referred to as the origin of sin. Today, we tend to think in

In today's political jargon, this is referred to as "spin," in which both sides of the current political tug-of-war show little willingness to accept truth or responsibility, and instead redirect the focus of the narrative elsewhere. Few engaged in political debate are willing to stay on point long enough to genuinely consider honest answers to the questions being posed to them. Each night, the televised evening news daily displays a limited number of "talking heads" who, when challenged, immediately change the subject and instead point fingers at their opponents.

The New Obsessional

In the 1970s, the cultural historian Christopher Lasch offered a poignant argument that America was becoming a culture of narcissism (Lasch, 1979) in which self-interest, entitlement, and instant gratification outstripped concerns for others and community. In director Oliver Stone's 1987 film *Wall Street,* the narcissistic anti-hero Gordon Gecko famously declares, "Greed is good."

Cultural narcissism is still alive and well in society but it is currently exhibiting a new facade, one that is properly termed *obsessional*. This appears to be the result of a convergence of factors, including increased existential insecurity, changes in moral values, social media that promotes "groupthink," and the influence of feminism and identity politics.

Obsessionals have limited access to their internal experience, especially to anger and other strong feelings. Freud referred to this as the obsessional's "isolation of affect." Avoidance is the behavioral strategy that obsessionals unconsciously adopt to limit potentially unpleasant confrontations with others, especially those who they perceive as in authority or able to criticize them.

Confrontation has always widely been viewed in civil society as un-

---

psychological terms rather than religious ones. But the term translated as "sin" in the Hebrew Bible is *cheyt*, which literally means "to miss the mark." It suggests being untrue to one's self. The path to healing is to return to one's "true self," as Winnicott referred to it.

pleasant and best avoided. The Judeo-Christian traditions view anger as either a "cardinal sin" or as best controlled. But there *are* situations that require its expression. The Rabbis suggested displays of anger in appropriate circumstances but without feeling out of control, because avoiding certain unpleasant situations that may require anger as a corrective is a mistake. In recent times, we have seen American leaders fail to confront threats and bad behaviors by countries such as North Korea, Iran, China, Russia, Saudi Arabia, etc., only to observe an increase in their threats and bad behavior.

But avoidance has become a staple of societal communication in America. It is possible to avoid real interactions with people by communicating primarily or even exclusively via social media. Political correctness is an obsessional behavioral strategy designed to control the anger of others while allowing one's own anger to remain unnoticed and undisturbed.

Chaos and Order

Obsessional neurosis is rooted in an archetypal motif that characterizes the natural struggle between "chaos" and "order." The structuring of chaos is an ancient motif of creation myths, including that of Genesis, in which God orders primordial chthonic forces via the imposition of language, or as the Prologue to the Gospel of John suggests, through the rational *Logos*. The imposition of thought on primitive emotions is a strategy widely adopted by society, and by obsessionals in the extreme.

In ancient times, the emergence of disruptive forces was symbolized by untamable waters (e.g., the Flood). Sacrifices and prayers were directed at divine forces to ensure their containment. In modern times, obsessional strategies have emerged to counter a perceived increase in existential dangers. Those elements in society that once fostered security have largely disappeared. Stable long-term employment is uncommon today; the average time that a family lives in the same house is less than four years. Religious beliefs that used to promote meaning in people's lives have been undermined by secularism and science. The philosopher Iddo Landau (2017) writes:

Attribution of value presupposes some worldview or categorization of how things are or should be, of what is of value and what is not. A loss in comprehension undermines the attribution of value, and then one feels meaninglessness. (Landau, p. 13)

There are new fears of cancer-producing environmental pollution and natural disasters attributable to global warming. The idea of psychological "trauma" as a precedent to mental dysfunction has become widespread, with increased fears of doing harm to others. Indeed, Freud recognized that obsessional neurotics express undue concern about harming others and attributed this to their repressed hostile feelings toward others.

Calls for progress, control, and efficiency are the all too common demands of the modern workplace, but also all standard obsessional preoccupations. It is virtually impossible to ignore the incessant demands of the workplace, friends, family, and the news cycle. E-mail, texting, and various social media platforms have resulted in a new normal of being "on-call" 24/7. This produces stress and heightened anxieties, which in turn tend to elicit obsessional defenses. As recently noted in BBC News (Newport, 2015):

We are the distracted generations, wasting hours a day checking irrelevant emails and intrusive social media accounts. And this "always on" culture – exacerbated by the smartphone – is making us more stressed and less productive, according to some reports. "Something like 40% of people wake up, and the first thing they do is check their email," says Professor Sir Cary Cooper of Manchester Business School, who has studied e-mail and workplace stress. "For another 40%, it's the last thing they do at night."

Digital technologies that can monitor the activities of literally all Americans are currently increasingly being employed to do so. This serves in part to achieve the omnipotent control that obsessionals desire, rationalized as a need for increased security.

But what is lost on the obsessional mind is its fundamentally irrational nature. Obsessionals will adamantly deny the extremity of their positions or admit they make little sense. Rather, they insist on their superior rationality and on the correctness of their positions. But when their arguments are scrutinized, the truth is evident to those who are not like-minded. For example, arguing for the "rights" of *criminal* illegal aliens at the expense of the safety of American citizenry is not rational. It increases the risk of harm in society. Excessive focus on the virtues of diversity and multiculturalism for its own sake is also *not* rational if it can be factually demonstrated that it fosters divisive identity politics and places American citizens at a disadvantage. But the question remains: If obsessionals are not in fact motivated by rational thinking, what *is* motivating them?

An Unconscious Society

Sigmund Freud recognized that behaviors are largely determined by motives beyond consciousness, by what he termed unconscious "drives" (*Trieb* in German). Freud was interested in how society participated in the repression of ideas and feelings. He viewed himself as a reformer, intent on freeing individuals from the prevailing repression of the Victorian age. As he argued in *Civilization and its Discontents*, the unconscious "wishes" of the unconscious invariably must conflict with the civilizing goals of society (S Freud, 1930). The socialization process requires that parents and the educational system impose constraints on the instincts of the child. The dilemma is how best to achieve the optimal balance between instinct and restraint. Freud opined that:

> Man is fundamentally antisocial. Society must domesticate him, must allow some satisfaction of biological-and hence ineradicable-drives; but for the most part society must refine and adroitly check man's basic impulses. In consequence of this suppression of natural impulses by society something miraculous happens: the suppressed drives turn into strivings that are culturally valuable and thus become

the human basis for culture. (Freud, *Civilization*, p. 8)

He envisioned a society in which the individual's instincts were controlled but not overly repressed, one that might result in a stable but creative society. Extremes of strictness or permissiveness undermine this goal. Freud's notion of *sublimation,* what he viewed as the highest psychological accomplishment, was that instinctual impulses would be transformed into societally acceptable creativity.

In his early *topographical* model of mind, Freud suggested that the primary unconscious drive was a sexual one, aimed at pleasure and necessary for procreation and the survival of the species. As Frank Sulloway concludes in *Freud: Biologist of the Mind*, like other scientists of his time, Freud was influenced by Darwin's competitive vision of survival of the fittest (Sulloway, 1979). Freud viewed sex as the primal drive that served the aims of evolution. While Freud's emphasis on Eros is often misconstrued by some as limited to physical sexuality, in fact, he was well aware of its broad symbolic implications, and he used the term to apply to a diversity of nonsexual behaviors as well. By 1920, in response to the events of the Great War and masochistic behaviors that appeared to defy the "pleasure principle" he observed in analysis, Freud concluded that *aggression* must be a second innate human drive (S Freud, 1923).

Few psychoanalytical theorists today are classical Freudians. Most have broadened their understanding of unconscious motivations to include a focus on affiliative behaviors, as important innate determinants of human behavior. Successful attachment to early caretakers is a universal feature of infancy, and one absolutely required for survival (Bowlby, 1969). But early attachments are subject to distortions due to repeated microtraumas or gross deficiencies in caretaking. Psychoanalytical theorists have argued that a variety of anxiety-driven attachment styles are causally associated with adult psychopathologies and that these in turn contribute to relational failures and to intergenerational attachment dysfunction. Wittgen et al. (2015) have demonstrated that *insecure* and *avoidant* attachment styles predict the appearance of adult obsessional personality traits.

Correlations between attachment anxiety/avoidance with specific obsessional personality disorder diagnostic criteria revealed that attachment avoidance was correlated with four of eight obsessional personality disorder criteria across the full sample. Within the subset of obsessional personality disorder patients, attachment avoidance was significantly correlated with obsessional personality disorder criterion excessively devoted to work and productivity to the exclusion of leisure activities and friendship. (Wittgen et al., p. 412)

Avoidance is the primary relational strategy of the obsessional.

An explanatory model of societal neurosis must account for the forces that promote and disrupt interpersonal affiliation, but it also optimally should include a consideration of those motives that are unconscious (i.e., unknown to the individual and by extension to larger groups) as well. As the psychoanalyst Erich Fromm contended, a social psychology that ignores unconscious factors risks missing critical underlying societal influences (Fromm, 1960). But as these are not openly expressed, experience is required to intuit accurately what may be driving behavior. An example of how critical psychological expressions can be guised is seen in *alexithymia* (i.e., the inability to "read" one's own feelings), a phenomenon that has become recognized increasingly in society (Sifneos, 1996).

Alexithymia

In Japanese culture, behaviors that were until recently casually accepted in the West have traditionally been considered "shameful." If one were to inquire of a Japanese man how he *feels* in what he perceives to be an uncomfortable social situation, one can expect a polite response and one seemingly devoid of apparent discomfort. However, when researchers monitored facial expressions and physiological responses closely for evidence of distress (e.g., increased heart rate, respiratory rate, skin resistance), they discovered that Japanese subjects were experiencing substantial stress that was not reported.

This type of physiological monitoring is the basis of the polygraph, or "lie detector" test. However, to conclude that the subject's response is consciously disingenuous is likely inaccurate. Rather, the evidence suggests that he was, at best, dimly aware of what he is feeling (Sartoru, 2016).

Alexithymic individuals exhibit difficulties identifying, describing, and reporting their feelings. A degree of alexithymia is present in virtually all rigid personality styles, and most commonly in obsessionals. Psychodynamically, these individuals exhibit a largely impermeable barrier between their conscious and unconscious experience. Some investigators have attributed this to a neuronal block in transferring impulse information from the right to the left cerebral hemispheres, but this may be an oversimplification. But as clinical experience confirms, obsessionals also show a defect in perceiving their own feelings and those of others as well (Vanheule, Desmet, Meganck, & Bogaerts, 2007). The Tin Woodman in Frank Baum's *The Wonderful Wizard of Oz,* who thinks well enough but is structurally rigid and lacks a "heart," is a poignant image of the alexithymic individual (Baum, 1900).

To what extent this is due to diminished innate capacities versus the result of developmental trauma cannot currently be answered accurately. One study examining alexithymia in subjects with obsessive-compulsive disorder found that higher alexithymia levels were associated with a gene that encodes an enzyme that degrades the neurotransmitter dopamine (Koh, Kang, Namkoong, Lee, & Kim, 2016). A study of Japanese males found higher scores on the Toronto Alexithymia Scale (Kano et al., 2012). But it is not possible to assess how much of this trait is genetically determined versus acquired by traumatic experience.

Projection: The Problem Is Not Me. It's You!

The psychoanalyst Carl Jung argued that the greatest problem facing modern man is an inability to recognize and assume responsibility for his unconscious feelings, because otherwise they are prone to be *projected* onto others. As Jung wrote:

> Just as we tend to assume that the world is as we see it, we naïvely suppose that people are as we imagine them to be. … All the contents of our unconscious are constantly being projected into our surroundings, and it is only by recognizing certain properties of the objects as projections or *imagoes* that we are able to distinguish them from the real properties of the objects. … *Cum grano salis*, we always see our own unavowed mistakes in our opponent. Excellent examples of this are to be found in all personal quarrels. Unless we are possessed of an unusual degree of self-awareness we shall never see through our projections but must always succumb to them, because the mind in its natural state presupposes the existence of such projections. It is the natural and given thing for unconscious contents to be projected. (Jung, "General Aspects of Dream Psychology," par. 507)

Projection is not a recent psychological discovery. It was well known to the moralists of antiquity. In Matthew 7, Jesus remarks, "How is it that you recognize the speck in your brother's eye and fail to see the beam in your own." This is an excellent description of projection that also hints at its moral complications.

Jung describes projection as a mental process that requires both a source and a recipient who can provide the "hook" for it. It is an unconscious dialogue in which both parties participate, albeit to varying degrees. The source of the projection is primarily responding to internal pressures. But without the "hook," the projection could not succeed. For example, if one has repressed anger, should events transpire that threaten to release that anger, it will be projected onto someone whose potential to be angered is somehow recognizable. The same scenario applies to repressed racism, bigotry, envy, etc.

However, projection is not simply a psychological mode of purging unacceptable intrapsychic contents. It is also an integral feature of learning. When one encounters someone, or something, that one has not previously observed, projections are automatically evoked. Like nature, the human psyche abhors a vacuum, and it automatically tends to project its known experience onto people, things, and situations (R. Kradin, 2007):

> In psychoanalytic thought, projection reflects a defense of the ego in which mental contents are unconsciously transferred onto others. Personality styles that include rigidly defended ego states are characterized by excessive reliance on projection. Freud referred to the patient's projections onto the analyst as transference and recognized that the abstinence of the analyst tended to promote transference projections. Jung recognized that projection is an archetypal psychological activity that is activated by insufficient knowledge of one's environment, including others. (Kradin, *Minding*, p. 1)

Imagine encountering a space alien for the first time. Depending on your predisposition, you might view it immediately as either harmful or harmless, angry and threatening or benevolent and well-meaning. With time, its nature may become clearer but only after you have had some time to observe it in action.

The Kleinian psychoanalyst Thomas Ogden has suggested that mentalization (i.e., the ability to think productively) develops from serial projections, which are subsequently "introjected" back into the source, in the service of achieving greater objectivity (Ogden, 2005). We project our own inner mental contents onto others but then reconsider our original predispositions based on new information. Unfortunately, for those with rigid personality traits, including obsessionality, narcissism, and paranoia, the re-collection of projections is defective. These personality types are unwilling to reconsider their fixed ideas. As a result, they are limited in their ability to learn new things and reassess both people and situations. The result is the persistence of perceptual distortions.

The dynamic that develops in psychoanalytic treatment, and what Freud suggested is the primary path to therapeutic change, is *transference.* In the analytical setting, the psychoanalyst, who is virtually unknown to the patient, over time becomes the object of repeated projections based on the patient's past relational experiences, in part driven by his or her wish to know more about the *real* analyst, with the aim of developing a secure attachment. As might be expected, these projections are at first distorted, although to the extent that the analyst's own psychology provides a "hook" for them, they will include a degree of truth.

In America, we are currently observing massive collective negative projections by obsessional Progressives onto President Trump, a man they hardly know, except in their own imaginings, but have uniformly judged as "evil." I do not know the president either, and I have seen many things about his personality that are off-putting to me. But I have also observed what appears to be a level of genuine concern and even warmth. I am still learning about the man. But I have met many Progressives who steadfastly refuse to consider his possible favorable traits. That does not strike me as fair or in the best interests of these individuals or the country.

Trump may be a large "hook," but he is not the problem. Rather, it is the disavowed hostility of these often "nice" people, who rather than reassessing their opinions of Trump's based on his actual behavior continue to resist integrating any information that does not accord with their preconceived ideas. From a psychoanalytical perspective, this can only be judged as a profound resistance and inability or stubborn unwillingness to learn. The object-relational psychoanalyst Melanie Klein described this psychological dynamic as the *paranoid-schizoid* position, and she noted that it was typical of primitive rigid personality types (Klein, 1958).

Rigid Progressives see the brash and egotistical new president as lacking in their own morally superior sense of humility. Trump's spontaneity and unpredictability cause them anxiety, due to fear of their own disavowed chaotic feelings. However, an objective observer would be hard pressed to identify a situation in which Trump has objectively done anything to merit the degree of fear reported by his opponents. Indeed, unconsciously, he may be everything that they covertly wish to be.

Their level of denial is confirmed by evidence that Progressives have shown an inability recently to assume responsibility for their own shortcomings. More than a year following defeat in her run for the presidency,

Hillary Clinton and her supporters are still intent on blaming their short-comings on a seemingly endless number of external factors, including unsubstantiated claims of electoral interference by Russia, lopsided media coverage, the actions of the former FBI director, computer hackers in Macedonia, etc. They choose to ignore the less comfortable fact that Mrs. Clinton was a poor candidate, a victim of her own numerous scandals who had miscalculated the discontent of America's voters with Barack Obama's policies and underrated the formidable populist message of her opponent.

Rigid obsessionals are invariably "sore losers," but the levels of unwillingness to accept defeat on both sides of the political spectrum suggest the apocalyptic levels of intense recalcitrance that we are witnessing today in society. There is a lesson for Americans in this; it comes from wisdom of Confucius: "The green reed which bends in the wind is stronger than the mighty oak which breaks in a storm." The growing level of rigid inflexibility in America does not portend well for its future.

Projected Racism

The frequent accusation that white men are guilty of misogyny and unconscious racism has repeatedly been raised to explain America's rejection of the policies of Barack Obama. In fact, "unconscious racism" is real; but it is also unavoidable, and it applies to everyone, not just Conservatives. The accusation is naive, as it ignores a critical, but for many an uncomfortable, biological fact. Modern neuroscience has repeatedly confirmed that the human brain automatically performs subliminal, or unconscious, evaluations of others. It is the *normal* role of the subcortical brain to scan the environment. The brain's lower and less highly evolved subcortical structures, including the amygdala and anterior cingulate gyrus, are actively engaged in identifying any environmental change or difference that could potentially pose a real threat.

In *Behavior: The Biology of Human Behavior at Its Best and Worst*, Robert Sapolsky notes that "the amygdala helps to mediate both innate and learned fear ... [injecting] implicit fear and distrust into social decision making" (Sapolsky, 2017)pp. 37-39). These automatic, near-instantaneous evaluations are subsequently reevaluated within the more recently evolved left frontal cortex by temporally slower pathways that are designed to make *rational* determinations with respect to whether the potential danger registered at subcortical levels should be acted on or not. Anyone who has owned a skittish cat will attest to how rapidly they react to what may in fact be no threat at all.

An example from daily human life may clarify this point. An urban American is likely to react initially fearfully to a group of young blacks wearing "hoodies" on a city street late at night. To not do so might potentially place oneself in *real* danger. Is this "bigotry" or "racism"? No, it is simply a rational response based on what is objectively known about crime statistics in America's cities, in which most violent urban crimes are in fact committed by young men of color. To deny facts in the service of an ideology is naïve or disingenuous. Human biology is what it is, as are the crime statistics in urban America, whether we think that they are fair or unfair, like them or not.

Biological evolution is glacial by comparison with the recent rapidity of social change. Jung recognized that this split between cognitive ideology and affective biology was a major cause of *neurosis* in modern society. We are unable to rise beyond our biology by wishful thinking. Moral progress is a perpetual struggle between our evolving neocortical structures and those lower centers that continue as part of our biological makeup. This is the struggle that Freud psychologized in metaphoric terms, because that's what psychology does, as the conflict between the Id and the Superego. One can tell oneself whatever story that one chooses to, but it will not make it true. As the late New York senator Daniel Patrick Moynihan used to say, "Everyone is entitled to his own opinion but not to his own facts." It is, in general, a mistake to ignore reality.

No one should be criticized for holding "prejudices," as they are as much a part of human nature as skin color, sex, or body habitus. No one should be held responsible for his innermost *feelings,* as they are invariably inaccessible. However, one can be culpable for choosing to speak them in public if they harm others, or consciously act upon them either to harm or to limit the freedom of others. The expectation of a world without bias is naïve, perfectionistic, and therefore neurotic.[20]

Openly repeated hostile accusations aimed at others are virtually always rooted in projections, and they are *prima facie* evidence of underlying characterological rigidity, and, when there is no evidence of insight, of severe personality disorder. Projections demonize others, and if unaddressed, lead to the scapegoating of innocents. The ancient notion of the "scapegoat" is based on ritualized transference projection. Leviticus 16 describes the ancient Israelite Day of Atonement, in which the sins of the people were ritually projected by the High Priest onto one of two identical goats, both without blemish.

One, the "scapegoat," was led into the wilderness and offered to a demonic spirit, whereas the other was sacrificed as an offering to God. This ritual was imagined to purge the sins of the people. Obviously, the goats were without sin, and that may at times be the case for people who are scapegoated as well. But before the ceremony was performed, the High Priest was required first to atone for himself and the people. Furthermore, atonement did not extend to those that men commit against each other. Those required asking forgiveness of the other and hoping that it was granted. The lesson should be clear: projection alone cannot effectively purge "sin"; only awareness and genuine atonement is effective. In secular terms, one must "own" one's projections.

I have tried in my arguments to remain even-handed. Both sides of the polarized populace are guilty at times of behaving badly. But I cannot ignore the vitriol that is broadcast over the airwaves nightly or posted on social media from the Progressive left. Yes, there is a lunatic right-wing

---

20 A colleague of mine recently told me that a relative who lives in Southern California is an administrator of a newly constructed hospital in San Diego. She told him that the new complex had been built in a northern suburb to reduce the number of illegal immigrants giving birth there. At the same time, the community encourages "open borders." It is difficult to know how to explain such decisions other than as hypocritical.

fringe, but they are just that, a fringe. The same can no longer be said about the left. They are currently either in power or chomping at the bit to be so. They are sadly no longer a fringe group.

Their incessant accusations of "racism" and "bigotry" are not only offensive to many, but they are also tedious. Like "the boy who cried wolf," one ceases to take whatever point they may have seriously. Their delivery is also in very bad "taste"; it lacks civility and sadly indicates how vicious American society has become.

Progressives should begin to realize that when they casually label others "racists" or "bigots," their behavior differs little from those who have demeaned Jews, blacks, and other minorities in the past. Therapists who have treated couples know that projections are the cause of the constant bickering that one observes in troubled marriages on the path toward divorce. The last time Americans went through a "divorce" was the Civil War. It was triggered by the election of another enormously unpopular president—Abraham Lincoln.

Projection versus Reality

The Jungian psychoanalyst Maria von Franz suggested that the accuracy of projections is ultimately determined by consensus (von Franz, 1985). In this vein, the author Gary Zukav (2012) argues:

> "Reality" is what we take to be true. What we take to be true is what we believe. What we believe is based upon our perceptions. What we perceive depends upon what we look for. What we look for depends upon what we think. What we think depends upon what we perceive. What we perceive determines what we believe. What we believe determines what we take to be true. What we take to be true is our reality. (Zukav, *Dancing*, p. 310)

Zukav's conclusion is in part correct but not entirely so. The social scientist Peter Berger, whose text the *Social Construction of Reality* was the source of much of the relativism that characterizes modern academic thought, registered his objections to the interpretation of his work by left-leaning scholars, in arguing for the "reality" of facts (Berger & Luckmann, 1966):

> Our concept of the social construction of reality in no way implies that there are no facts. Of course, there are physical facts to be determined empirically from the fact that a massacre took place to the fact that someone stole my car. But the very concept of objectivation implies that there are social facts as well, with a robust reality that can be discovered regardless of our wishes . . . but the various narratives . . . correspond very neatly with a definition of schizophrenia, when one can no longer distinguish between reality and one's fantasies. (Berger and Luckmann, *Social*, p. 133.)

What Berger describes as "schizophrenia" is more properly (psychologically speaking) termed *neurotic illusion,* although frankly delusional ideation has also become commonplace, its most recent manifestation in what has glibly been termed "Trump Derangement Syndrome."

As we have seen, the notion of truth as belief has become increasingly widespread. Emma Jung, Carl's wife and a psychoanalyst in her own right, described the propensity of women to make decisions based on how they feel about a matter rather than on facts. In *Anima and Animus,* she ascribed such opinions as *animus* opinions, "with fixed ideas, collective opinions and unconscious *a priori* assumptions that lay claim to absolute truth. In a woman who is identified with the animus (called animus-possession), Eros generally takes second place to Logos" (E. Jung, 1985) p. 57).

Unpacking the Jungian jargon, this means that for uncertain psychological reasons, some women express strong convictions based on feelings rather than logic, and then argue them in ways that undermine dialogue and cooperation. Jung ascribed this to a desire for power that outstripped the wish to promote relationship. Opinions based on subjective feelings with little or no basis in fact are widely observed today amongst both men and women. One may be entitled to an opinion, but that does not make it fact.

Certainly, both men and women are guilty of this, but women and minorities who are wielding power for the first time need to recognize that they are like young school children allowed to exercise power over each other. That exercise quickly degenerates, and adults must move in to put the situation back on track. Am I saying that white men need to return to power as was once uniformly the case? Obviously not, as those days are over. But as Emma Jung suggests in her text, the exercise of power needs to be cultivated. Those who have had little experience with it can at first use it erratically or become defensive if they think that they might lose it.

It is fair, even if politically incorrect, to suggest that both women and minorities may need to learn how to exercise power more judiciously than they are doing today. Indeed, I believe that amateurish approaches to freedom and power account for much of the uncivil tone in society today. We will not benefit as a society from those who are aggrieved by old grudges with white men. This comment does not merit my being attacked for being part of an old patriarchal establishment. That may be true, but it's not the point.

There is a clear parallel between the emergence of both feminism and the civil right movement in the 1960s and the level of societal conflict in America today. This must be acknowledged so that those who are now beginning to wield power can learn to do so wisely. Ranting and raving about Trump, racists, white men, and gun owners is not the way to conduct a dialogue that is likely to achieve one's ends. It is merely a huge turn-off for many. If groups desire to be respected, they are going to have to earn it, like everybody else had to. There is no free lunch.

Neurosis and Experience

According to the psychoanalyst David Shapiro in *Autonomy and Rigid Character* (Shapiro, 1981):

Neurosis in one way or another restricts subjective experience. Neurotic attitudes and ways of thinking having developed in shrinking or self-protective reaction to conflict or discomfort, then tend to inhibit the full conscious experience of conflictful and discomforting feelings or motivations. This is not merely the conscious experience of particular memories, feelings, or wishes that are inhibited, but whole classes of subjective experience that are inimical to these attitudes are also inhibited. (Shapiro, *Autonomy*, p. 54)

But to diagnose neurosis, which is an expression of an "unhealthy" mind, one must first be able to define mental health, and this is not an easy task. Some, like the late psychiatrist Thomas Szasz in the *Myth of Mental Illness,* have argued that psychopathology is primarily an "affectation" rather than a disease (Szasz, 2010). Indeed, the notion of psychopathology has in recent years evoked criticism, mostly by nonmedical psychotherapists, who view it as unnecessarily "stigmatizing." But while classifications of personality that are largely descriptive exist, it is virtually impossible to identify one that is devoid of implied pathology. It is simply not possible to develop a metapsychology for therapeutics that is not value laden. The pressing question, however, is *whose* values will be applied.

Physical health has been operationally defined by some as the adaptive plasticity of physiological activities in response to environmental change. A variety of homeostatic mechanisms serve to maintain bodily functions within defined limits (e.g., body temperature, blood sugar levels, etc.). These serve as thermostats, regulating activities around predetermined set points. Although the truth is somewhat more complex, the body is a self-regulating system that responds adaptively to environmental changes. From this perspective, physical disease may be defined as the nonadaptive response to change.

A comparable definition can be applied to mental health. Neurosis can from this perspective be defined as an overly limited response to a changing environment, comparable to Shapiro's definition of neurosis as "restricted experience" (Shapiro, 1981). Indeed, psychologists intuitively referred to "rigid personalities" and to the tendency amongst neurotics to repeat behaviors that are non-adaptive and ultimately self-defeating compulsively.

Erich Fromm suggested that mental health and the aims of a society are not necessarily overlapping (Fromm, 1960):

> The person who is healthy in terms of being well-adapted is often less healthy than the neurotic person in terms of human values. Often, the latter is well adapted only at the expense of having given up his self in order to become more or less the person he believes he is expected to be. All genuine individuality and spontaneity may have been lost.... [T]he neurotic person can be characterized as somebody who was not successful and instead of expressing his self productively, he sought salvation through neurotic symptoms and by withdrawing into phantasy life. Nevertheless, from the standpoint of human values, he is less crippled than the kind of normal person who has lost his individuality altogether. (Fromm, *Escape*, p. 138)

It is possible to be "normal" in a deranged society but one must be prepared to suffer, as did the Ugly Duckling in Hans Christian Andersen's fairy tale. This was the challenge that Freud confronted. He lived in a Victorian Europe whose repressed mores were considered the norm. He wished to transform society while fostering the individual's autonomy. When the demands of a society are overly rigid, neurotic styles ensue. Pressures are exerted on healthy individuals from an early age to conform via educational strategies of reward and punishment that target ideas, speech, and action. The success of such a society will be measured by conformity. In today's politically correct society, obsessional conformity is rewarded while genuine mental health is being increasingly punished.

Jung chose not to categorize psychopathology; he preferred a descriptive "phenomenological" model of personality typology that was devoid of historical explanations. He instead classified personalities as exhibiting extraverted (outer directed) or introverted (inner directed) attitudes, and polarized capacities for "thinking" versus "feeling," "intuition" versus "sensation" (*Psychological Types*, 1972). According to Jung, a well-adapted non-neurotic person exhibits a reasonable balance between these psychological attitudes and functions. Neurosis results from one-sided imbalances in the functional capacities of the psyche. Individuals with different typologies experience difficulties understanding each other, due to different modes of perception of their experience.

Only a limited number of contents can be held in the conscious field at the same time, and of these only a few can attain the highest grade of consciousness. The activity of consciousness is selective. Selection demands direction. But direction requires the exclusion of everything irrelevant. This is bound to make the conscious orientation one-sided. The contents that are excluded and inhibited by the chosen direction sink into the unconscious, where they form a counterweight to the conscious orientation. (Jung, *Psychological Types,* para. 694)

The obsessional shows a propensity for thinking and can be expected to differ in his assessments of reality from those with other personality types. This can lead to societal strife when the modes of perception in a society become limited and increasingly polarized.

A Culture of Therapy

Rieff suggests in *Triumph of the Therapeutic* that large swaths of modern society, influenced by superficial appreciations of psychoanalytical ideas, currently view themselves as "victimized" and in need of therapy. This is unfortunate, as it undermines the notion of mental health and tends to reduce assuming personal responsibility (Rieff, 1966). After all, what can mental health possibly mean when virtually everyone is "ill"? The phrase "It's not your fault," heard frequently today, is meant to comfort those who feel culpable for their misfortunes, but in fact that approach is not necessarily therapeutic. Rather, it tends to serve as a temporary balm while allowing individuals to avoid assuming responsibility for their actions as adults.

The ability to maintain neurosis requires persistent perceptual and interpretive distortions. When these become extreme and inflexible, they can achieve the level of delusion, and in the past those suffering from them were termed *psychotic*. The boundaries between neurosis and psychosis are permeable. Under conditions of stress, obsessional neurotic illusions can devolve into psychotic delusions, often of a paranoid type.

Chapter 6: The Obsessional Personality

Two roads diverged in a yellow wood,

And sorry that I could not travel both

And be one traveler, long I stood.

—Robert Frost. *The Road Not Taken*

Apocalyptic psychology is not a term that can be found in the nosology of psychiatry. A previously noted, the gods and many previously recognized religious categories of behavior have been secularized and pathologized as neuroses within psychiatric terminology. Neurotic styles in society exhibit features comparable to those of neurotic individuals. For this reason, it may be helpful to delineate how obsessionality typically manifests in individuals in their lives and in psychotherapy. Compulsiveness is the behavioral counterpart of obsessionality, and it is generally understood as a motoric path toward relieving anxiety (R. L. Kradin, 2004). Compulsions manifest as *excessive* work, cleaning, exercise, sexuality, drug or other addictions. Whereas most people share some of these behaviors, when extreme, they are properly termed obsessive-compulsive.

Obsessionality manifests along a spectrum of severity from obsessional style, to obsessional personality disorder (OPD) and severe obsessive-compulsive disorder (OCD) (Association, 1994). It is impossible to assess the true prevalence of obsessionality in society because it is thought that few seek psychiatric care and therefore elude enumeration. Indeed, many obsessionals at the workplace accept the "label" jokingly and with pride. They see the quest for perfection as valuable, and their ritualistic behaviors as benign idiosyncrasies.

However, the impact of obsessionals on society is substantial, particularly as they tend to gravitate toward positions of authority and power. They may excel at the workplace due to hard work and attention to detail. But their rigid workstyle can also lead to sterility, a preoccupation with unnecessary rules, minutiae, all eventually leading to stagnation. Their idea of "progress" tends to be focused primarily on procedural efficiency at the expense of creativity or novelty. When obsessionals come to clinical attention, it is generally because their levels of perfectionism or stubborn critical demeanor have disturbed co-workers or domestic relationships.

Jung referred to obsessionals as extraverted "thinking-sensation" types, emphasizing what he viewed as their dominant psychological functions (*Psychological Types*, 1972). In this schema, obsessionals are predicted to exhibit limited "feeling" and "intuition." Jung's system has descriptive power, but it does not address the range of behaviors that one encounters in obsessionals, nor does it choose to provide developmental explanations for this personality style.

Obsessional neurosis holds a privileged place in the history of psychopathology. Along with *hysteria*, it was one of the two major neurotic styles recognized prior to the advent of psychoanalysis. As Shapiro notes (Shapiro, 1981):

> Two neurotic modes of volitional action—that of hysterical and impulsive characters and certain passive "weak" individuals, and that of rigid character serve to illustrate the forms of conscious self-direction. Among the former aims are exceedingly vague and intentions are hardly articulated or self-conscious. Such a person may feel that he has no aims of his own, that his actions are entirely determined by force of circumstance or the expectations of others. . . . Among rigid characters on the other hand there is an extraordinary degree of articulation and self-consciousness of aim and purpose, an often-excruciating consciousness of choice and decision, and great deliberateness of action. (Shapiro, *Autonomy*, p. 18)

The hysterical style was seen in women, whereas obsessionality was considered a masculine style, in a time when gender differences were clearer and widely accepted as true.

The factors that contribute to the psychogenesis of obsessionality are uncertain, but genetics, developmental and sexual traumas, and cultural values may all contribute (*Diagnostic and Statistical Manual of Mental Disorders-V*, 2010). The previous edition of *Diagnostic and Statistical Manual of Mental Disorders* (DSM–IV) included obsessive-compulsive disorder (OCD) as an anxiety disorder, emphasizing the cardinal role that it plays in its symptomatology. Indeed, phobias and generalized anxiety are frequent co-morbidities in those with obsessional styles. The current nosology of psychopathology, DSM-5, has removed OCD from within the category of anxiety disorders and distinguishes it from the more common and less disabling obsessional personality disorder (OPD). Nevertheless, the symptoms and behaviors of those with OCD and OPD exhibit substantial overlap, and it can be impossible to distinguish the two at times.

As Shapiro notes, obsessional personality is part of a psychodynamic spectrum of "rigid personality disorders," which includes obsessional, narcissistic, and paranoid styles, and these can also be difficult to distinguish in practice (Shapiro, 1981). However, the grandiosity of the narcissist is covert in those who have obsessional traits, and narcissists are far more prone to react with openly expressed anger when they perceive that they have been slighted. What both share from a psychodynamic perspective is a largely impermeable barrier between ego-consciousness and their feelings. Both are hypersensitive to criticism, exhibit difficulties in regulating self-esteem, and are prone to projective defenses that exteriorize disavowed "flaws" onto others, rather than taking responsibility for them (Salzman, 1977).

Freud's Structural Model of the Psyche

Early in his career as a psychoanalyst, Freud noted that the obsessional shares features with the young child by insisting on perfection and via imagined "omnipotence of thought." In his theorizing on obsessional neurosis in the *Rat Man* and *Notes Upon a Case of Obsessional Neurosis* (1909d), Freud suggested that conflicted feelings of love and hate for early caretakers were the source of obsessional ambivalence, doubt, and compulsion. In *Inhibitions, Symptoms and Anxiety* (S Freud, 1959a), he described the main defense mechanisms of obsessional neurosis as *avoidance of affect* and the *undoing of actions*, the latter reflected by an inability to make firm decisions without doubt or regret and efforts at undoing them.

Freud's *structural model* of the psyche divided the mind into (1) a conscious *ego* (I) that mediates between the interior and external milieu and is the seat of conscious attention, (2) an unconscious *id* (It) that is the seat of instinctual drives, and (3) a *superego* (conscience) that represents incorporated societal mores. The superego actively seeks to repress "negative" thoughts and feelings so that they remain at best dimly perceived by the obsessional. This serves to reduce the anxiety that threatens to overwhelm the obsessional ego and fosters the illusion of control. Freud remarked: "The poor ego has a still harder time of it; it has to serve three harsh masters, and it has to do its best to reconcile the claims and demands of all three.... The three tyrants are the external world, the superego, and the id" (S Freud, 1933).

The rigid boundary between conscious and unconscious domains is recapitulated in the obsessional's relationships with others. He may be exceedingly polite and even outgoing but at the core is reserved and affectually "cool." Intellectual defenses are used to ward off others, and commitments and physical intimacy tend to be avoided.

Anxiety

When probed obsessionals report anxiety as a persistent *background affect*. Some report free-floating anxiety with no obvious source; others have specific phobias. When psychoanalyzed, these anxieties can be traced to fears of being overwhelmed in childhood, difficulties maintaining boundaries, and fears of physical injury, mental dissolution, and death (Salzman, 1977). Anxiety is rapidly countered by compulsive activities, but it soon returns once activities cease.

Cognition is the path to restraining negative affects, most notably anger. Thought promoting strategies are part of the normal socialization project of controlling anger in childhood. But the obsessional, as Fromm suggests, has been overly socialized and covertly resents it (Fromm, 1960). They show an affinity for "rational" thought, choose their words with care, and may become enamored with language. Although they may be highly intelligent, the rationales they adopt to explain themselves are defensive; they are meant to deceive and to obscure their anxieties from conscious awareness.

The extremity of their concerns is well beyond what at least until recently would have been accepted as the norm. The following example highlights this point:

A young obsessional man in his teens suffered from a fear of developing cancer and would assiduously avoid all activities that might expose him to carcinogens, including the sun, ambient air pollution, and the basement of the family house for fear of being exposed to radon, a known cause of lung cancer. When family and friends suggested that his fears were extreme and unreasonable, he countered that *no* risk was worth taking and suggested that others would be well advised to adopt his position as well.

Although accurate in theory, most well-adjusted individuals are not this fearful. Yes, there are risks related to excessive sun exposure, but on balance efforts at eliminating them altogether would greatly limit one's freedom. But this mode of rationalization is the primary cognitive defense of the obsessional, and it is extremely difficult to divest them of it. Rather than accept that their ideas are extreme and irrationally fearful—a first and necessary step for achieving real change—the obsessional will proceed to invent additional rationales for his behavior. Complex rituals may develop to ward off perceived dangers can result in the production of an imaginal cocoon out of which the obsessional refuses to emerge.

Unfortunately, such fearful concerns have become commonplace in society. They manifest as excessive anxieties concerning health, environmental pollution, global warming, the policing of impolitic speech, appearing prejudiced, fear of being sexually harassed or of being perceived as a harasser, etc. The list of societal concerns appears to be ever increasing. But when perfectionistic control becomes the mantra of a society, it has become neurotic, not better.

Shame

Admitting to being fearful is shaming for the obsessional. Shame is always accompanied by efforts at concealment, and the endless rationalizations of the obsessional are a subterfuge meant to avoid feeling shamed. Those obsessionals who refuse to consider that their fears are excessive are referred to as having "limited insight," a poor prognostic sign in treatment (*Diagnostic and Statistical Manual of Mental Disorders-V*, 2010).

A 50-year-old man entered therapy with the goal of knowing more about himself. He insisted that he was not interested in exploring his past or any dystonic feelings that he might be experiencing, despite having a host of problems in his life, including many compulsive activities. After several sessions, he announced that he had been giving matters a lot of thought on his own and now understood himself, so would no longer require treatment.

Restricted Affect

At a granular level, it is impossible to think and feel simultaneously. The non-neurotic mind fluidly alternates between thinking and feeling, whereas compulsive thinking reinforces the obsessional's restriction of affect. But it would be wrong to conclude that the obsessional is necessarily a "cold" character. In some contexts, he may exhibit extraordinary sentimentality. One obsessional male patient of mine was routinely moved to tears at parades and weddings. Others exhibit extraordinary sympathy toward those whom they perceive as disadvantaged. But in truth, this primarily represents a projection of their own disavowed feelings of rejection and abandonment.

The cool persona of the obsessional often can often be traced to a childhood in which they were thrust into an adult parental role prematurely. Obsessionals give the impression of independence and competence, and they may be at the workplace or in managing their home. But they complain of feeling easily overwhelmed, and they fear abandonment in close relationships. They become resentful and spiteful when their needs are not attended to by others.

A 54-year-old man was highly successful professionally. He came to analysis with marital difficulties complaining that his wife was "cold" and unsupportive. Within the family, he often assumed the role of concerned caretaker for his young children and accused his wife of neglecting them. He was angry with his wife and resentful of feeling misunderstood and unrewarded by others, despite his success. He prided himself on being hyper-responsible but always felt on the verge of being overwhelmed and resented having to attend to the needs of others. He approached his divorce as another issue that needed to be managed but recognized that something was missing in his "heart."

Anger

Freud recognized that the obsessional is angry with authority but also takes great pains to conceal it, even from himself. In many cases, one encounters a developmental scenario in which anger directed at caretakers was either rebuffed or responded to in turn with anger, guilt, shaming behaviors, or abandonment. The parental home is often described as perfectionistic, controlled, and a place where autonomy was discouraged. Contradictory and confusing parental displays of enabling and abandoning behaviors are commonly described. In other cases, the home environment may have been so chaotic that all the child's energies were necessarily directed at maintaining order. In such cases, obsessional features may alternate with chaotic behaviors.

L. was raised by parents who both exhibited severe obsessional traits. Perfectionism was the mode in her rule-bound home and polite behavior without displays of anger were insisted upon. Whereas L. viewed her father as nurturing, analysis revealed that he was highly controlling and had persistently resisted L.'s efforts to act independently. Her mother was described as critical, distant, and prone to abandoning L. if she expressed any signs of anger.

This mode of parenting makes it extremely difficult for children to discern that they are being controlled and that their autonomy was secretly undermined. As adults, they alternate between being reliant on authority and at odds with it. Stable attachments and mature intimacy in adult relationships can be difficult to maintain.

Repressed anger at caregivers is carried into adulthood, and relationships to authority are often conflicted. This manifests as a dynamic in which anger is expressed via sadistic modes of control, alternating with masochistic positions (Shapiro, 1981). Sadomasochistic attachments are maintained until no further attachment benefit can be gleaned from them.

Anger is repressed and may be virtually impossible to access. Some obsessionals exhibit exceptionally gentle personas. But what is commonly observed are unconsciously driven passive-aggressive strategies aimed at frustrating and evoking anger of those who they perceive as being more powerful. This is achieved by what the child psychoanalyst Melanie Klein referred to as *projective identification* (Ogden, 2005). When this strategy is successful, it manages to disavow feelings of anger while evoking them in others. One can often detect a faint sadistic smile on the face of the obsessional patient when he thinks that he has somehow angered or diminished others (Reich, 1962).

In public and in the presence of authority, the obsessional is polite and even obsequious. But the attuned analyst can discern hints of anger in the form of subtle insults or facial expressions that reflect their feelings of contempt (Reich, 1962). One obsessional patient of mine would routinely crumple the check that he used for the session's payment before handing it to me, a manifestation of his otherwise well-guised contempt.

The adult obsessional compulsively reenacts the parental demand of behaving like a "nice" boy or girl. Indeed, this persists into adulthood and can become so overbearing as to eclipse all other concerns. One moody obsessional young man would smile when being photographed, and then instantly revert to being unpleasant with his family. Around friends and strangers, he was consistently polite, gentle, enthusiastic, and "politically correct." At home, he was rude, sullen, and profoundly passive-aggressive. In public, the obsessional is careful to display inordinate sensitivity toward the feelings of others and may be widely viewed as "compassionate" or as a "really nice guy." But as Shapiro notes, these behaviors are in fact neurotic, and they do not represent the genuine feelings of the obsessional:

> What makes the conscientiousness of the compulsive person special is different from the nature or the strength of his values, standards, or purposes...When the compulsive person reminds himself that he should do something because it is the right thing, the nice thing, or the generous thing, he is prompted not by kindness, generosity, or concern for justice but by a sense of rules and duties to do something kind, generous, or nice. (Shapiro, *Autonomy*, p. 80)

In private, the obsessional may be willing to criticize others, especially those who do not share his values. He may adopt punitive measures toward others, when he knows that they cannot be traced directly back to him. A highly obsessional young man was showered with faint praise by his peers as being the "least likely to confront anyone." Attempts at avoiding confrontation may include deceitful behaviors. Politicians at all levels of governance are well known for this strategy; they are practiced at deception in the service of avoiding confrontation and maintaining control. The expectation of honesty in politics is virtually an oxymoron. Few obsessionals are brave; most are cowards.

In institutional settings, acting as part of a group is the preferred mechanism for obsessionals to express their hostility without fear of being singled out for retribution or being viewed publicly as "mean." In groups, obsessionals strive to create a "civil" environment of polite but shallow interactions. Kindness, a genuine virtue, is for the obsessional an imperative, as well as a meta-communication of personal vulnerability and hypersensitivity. These strategies underlie the psychology of "political correctness" and explain why it has had broad appeal in obsessional society. When taken to the extreme, as it is in classrooms and workplaces, "political correctness" limits the ability to teach and learn effectively. As Hillel, a Talmudic sage observed in the *Ethics of the Fathers*, "the overly sensitive student cannot learn" (Lau, 2007).

Doubt

The neuroscientist Antonio Damasio suggests that the normal decision-making process requires knowing how one *feels* about the choice (Damasio, 2000). On a cautionary note, feelings are not the same as emotions; they are, instead, rational evaluations with respect to what is likely to be beneficial or not *vis-à-vis* the self. The capacity to make decisions is a *sine qua non* of genuine autonomy. But the obsessional is limited in this capacity by an inability to know how he feels. When one takes a detailed developmental history, one finds that decisions were made for the obsessional with little opportunity for the exercise of free will. Consequently, he may renege on decisions, fearful of having made the wrong one, or continue to look to others to make choices for him. The latter may be an older parental figure or a peer group. When no alternative is available, the obsessional tends to procrastinate.

The classical example of obsessional preoccupation in literature is Shakespeare's *Hamlet*, in which the protagonist struggles throughout the play trying to decide how and when to act to avenge his father's murder and the usurpation of what was rightfully his throne. Consider the following example from psychoanalytical practice:

A 40-year-old obsessional woman needed to replace her old car, which was in the shop for repairs more often than not. For more than a year, she researched automobiles, looking for the "perfect choice." But each time she came close to deciding, she became paralyzed by doubt. After two years, she precipitously purchased a car that lacked most of the features she had been searching for.

This mode of manic decision making is also common for obsessionals. Eventually, unable to tolerate the anxiety that accompanies being paralyzed by doubt, they make a sudden decision that does not serve them well, simply to get it out of the way. Freud recognized this failure to commit as a common feature of obsessionality.

Perfectionism

The obsessional is a perfectionist. But because "to err is human," obsessionals are prone to implosions of self-esteem when their flaws are revealed. To maintain the illusion of perfection, the obsessional must assiduously avoid criticism. Exceptionally "thin skinned," they may recognize imperfections in others, but not in themselves. Alternatively, they may be excessively humble, quick to criticize themselves, and prone to ignore the faults of others. The latter strategy is invariably a ruse meant to produce the image of being "kind." In some cases, their level of narcissistic absorption does not allow them even to register the faults of others.

Perfectionism is a sign of psychological immaturity. The obsessional resembles Jean Piaget's description of the six-year-old child who believes in perfection and the magical omnipotence of his thoughts (Piaget, 1960). Indeed, the analysis of the obsessional uncovers puerile inclinations in many sectors of psychological experience. For example, whereas they are often serious without much of a sense of humor, they may be amused by "bathroom humor" and by puns.[21]

---

21   The letters of Wolfgang Amadeus Mozart to his father, Leopold, and to his own wife

A patient described his father as a severely obsessional personality. When the child was young, they would watch cartoons on television together. But after the age of six or seven, the child grew tired of the silly images while his father continued to watch the cartoons by himself, chuckling all the while at what the boy had grown to view as inane.

Obsessional hypersensitivity to criticism leads to diminished risk taking and diminished creativity. Their intense self-scrutiny and impossibly high standards result in a pervasive lack of joy, a state referred to as *anhedonia*, or the inability to enjoy life.

Cleanliness

Most are acquainted with obsessionals who profess a preoccupation with cleanliness. The classic example is the housewife who cleans compulsively, making certain that nothing "foreign" contaminates the purity of her domicile, or the patient with OCD who exhibits compulsive hand washing. For some obsessionals, the concern is expressly with "dirt," for others it is exposure to germs, but these preoccupations can overlap. The deeper underlying concerns include contamination, illness, and death.

Obsessionals create boundaries to secure their well-being. One can imagine this unconscious strategy as a fractal that iterates itself repeatedly at different scales of experience.[22] The desire to purge the world of "dirt" extends to various levels of experience. Political correctness includes purging speech of "dirty" words and "negative" phrases. However, even the radical Progressive Saul Alinsky bristled at the idea of expunging words with unpleasant connotations, and he rejected efforts at sterilizing speech. As he complains in *Radicals: A Primer for Realistic Radicals* (Alinsky, 1971):

Let us look at the word *power*. *Power* meaning "ability, whether phys-

---

include numerous allusions to bathroom activities and the extensive inclusion of puns.

22　A fractal is a self-reiterating function, much like a tree that continues to branch at both larger and smaller levels.

ical, mental, or moral, to act," has become an evil word, with overtones and undertones that suggest the sinister, the unhealthy, the Machiavellian. . . . [T]he word *power* is mentioned as though hell has been opened, exuding the stench of the devil's cesspool of corruption. It evokes images of cruelty, dishonesty, selfishness, arrogance, dictatorship, and abject suffering. The word *power* is associated with conflict; it is unacceptable in our present Madison Avenue deodorized hygiene, where conflict is blasphemous and the value is being liked and not offending others. *Power*, in our minds, has become almost synonymous with corruption and immorality. (Alinsky, *Primer*, p. 51)

One could not ask for a better summary of the hypersensitive concerns of the obsessional Progressive. Power, contamination, politeness—Alinsky touches on all their major concerns. Alinsky's famous mentees, Barack Obama and Hillary Clinton, apparently missed this point, as Alinsky's direct approach to language more closely approximates that of Donald Trump.

Fixed ideas

The *idée fixee* was originally recognized as a feature of obsessionality. The afflicted person is unable to resist a train of thought. In neurosis, compulsive thoughts may be recognized as irrational, whereas in psychosis they are accepted without dispute, and the individual cannot be moved from his belief. In the recent presidential election, it was commonplace for those on the left to accuse Donald Trump of being a "racist." Despite repeated denials and little credible evidence to support their claim, they could not be swayed. To claim that half of America is currently frankly delusional may sound ludicrous. But the fact is that such fixed ideas suggest a severe degree of psychological distortion that is at least severely neurotic.

An obsessional woman in her early 30s was the daughter of an Italian American physician who died suddenly when she was in her 20s. She recalled many fond moments with her father but was disturbed by what she viewed as his "racism." She had a propensity to date African-American men, who often were far less intelligent and accomplished than herself. When I suggested that perhaps her choice of partners might be unconsciously driven by anger toward her father, she became irate and quit analysis, suggesting that she could not work with a "racist."

This patient was undoubtedly correct in suggesting that her father held racial prejudices, as these were common and at times overtly expressed in his generation. But she was unable to provide any example in which he had acted in discriminatory way toward people of color. This distinction between thought and action is critical. In most societies, it is a fundamental tenet of law that only actions are subject to punishment. But today's politically correct society is rapidly approaching George Orwell's totalitarian *1984,* in which "thought crimes"[23] were also subject to punishment (Orwell, 1950). Whereas prejudicial speech *is* disturbing in a liberal society based on the right to free speech, it should be permissible. At a minimum, one must reserve the right to harbor private thoughts without recriminations. We are all guilty of less than glowing opinions of some people or groups, and to hold individuals to impossible standards reflects a level of perfectionism that is unreasonable.[24] As the political commentator David Horowitz suggests in *Progressive Racism*:

---

23   The basis of this may be traced to early Christianity. Many of the sayings attributed to Jesus in his Sermon on the Mount in Matthew and the Sermon on the Plain in Luke extend the transgression of the law from a mode of action to a mode of thought. The usual motif is that "you have been taught x, but I say y," with y being a more extreme element linked to thought preceding action. Sin becomes not merely a behavioral transgression but a thought crime. A modern example is President Jimmy Carter's statement during an interview that he often "sinned in his heart."

24   In the opening discussion of the eighteenth-century text *Tanya* by the first *Rebbe* of Chabad Hassidism, there is a lengthy discussion of what constitutes a pure *Tzaddik*, or righteous man, and a *beinoni*, an in-between man. Both observe the Law perfectly and are indistinguishable to an observer. They differ in that the pure *Tzaddik* no longer has any inclination toward sin. It is noted that such people are extremely rare. To hold individuals to such an impossible standard leads to self-loathing and intolerance, and one is chided not to think of oneself as a "bad person" lest one become depressed and unable to live a joyful life.

To achieve the benevolent outcomes that progressives promise would require a government both omniscient and wise, a utopia that has never existed. Such a state would have to mandate comprehensive strategies of opportunity and wealth, and would conduct a relentless battle against human nature to overcome the resistance to its impositions by those unwilling to give up their liberty or the fruits of their labor.... The level playing field requires a totalitarian state to eliminate the disparities resulting from human nature and private circumstance. (Horowitz, *Progressive*, p. 57)

Indeed, one of the most disturbing features of the current Progressive agenda is its increasing tendency to merge thought, speech, and action into a singular monolithic taboo on an ever-increasing range of topics.

This young woman was not devoid of her own prejudices, but unfortunately her hypersensitivities precluded the possibility of exploring them, a process that she potentially might have benefited from. But her mindset has become the norm for many Progressive Millennials[25] as consequence of a systematic indoctrination into Progressive ideas in schools, messages communicated through the mainstream media, the music they listen to, and the opinions of their peers on social media. Efforts at preserving individual rights are routinely challenged in Progressive society:

A young woman was approached by a black man for a date. For a variety of personal reasons, she refused. She was subsequently accused by the man and by her own friends of being a "racist" and pressured to go out on the date. She still refused, but was deeply hurt by the experience.

Envy and Schadenfreude

Perfection is not an achievement that the obsessional easily shares with others. He is prone to being envious of others who are successful. This psychological state is referred to as *schadenfreude*, which is the in-

---

25 Millennials are poorly defined as those who will become adults in the early twenty-first century, including those born between the late 1980s and 2000.

clination to demean anything good that happens to others.

A highly intelligent and obsessional young man applied and was accepted to an Ivy League college. However, when he learned that his best friend had been accepted at the school of *his* choice, he was visibly upset and insisted that he could not have been accepted to an Ivy League university without the help of a financial "bribe" by his wealthy parents. He himself had been accepted as a "legacy" student.

This lack of generosity toward others is symptomatic of the pettiness often exhibited by obsessionals.

Aversion to Risk

Plagued by existential anxieties, the obsessional is risk averse. He avoids situations that are without clear and safe outcomes. Having said this, they may also be paradoxically inclined to take unnecessary risks, apparently in reaction to their own natural cautiousness. The mountain climber and journalist Jon Krakauer described his own obsessional character and how it drove him to take what most would agree were exceptional risks (Krakauer, 1999).

The cautious obsessional may be agoraphobic, fearing to journey far from the safety of home and envious of those who do take risks. Rather than admit that others are less fearful, which would suggest their own inadequacy, the obsessional is instead highly critical of risk takers, preferring to view them as "brash" or "cavalier." Should the risk taker succeed, he is judged "lucky," as the obsessional is faint with praise. On the other hand, should a risk taker fail, the judgment that "he got what he deserved" is swift. Some of the aversion to Donald Trump expressed by obsessionals is attributable to his risk taking, which they view as dangerous or incompetent, even though he has proven repeatedly to be successful. But what they cannot admit is that they are in fact *envious* of his enormous and unexpected success.

Trump embodies what Jungian psychologists refer to as *trickster* qualities. He is mercurial and difficult to pin down. One is reminded of the mythic encounter between Hermes, the *trickster*, and his half-brother Apollo, the Greek god of structure and order:

Shortly after his birth Hermes craved meat and devised a scheme for stealing the cattle of Apollo. He butchered two of the cattle and divided rich parts of the meat into twelve portions, which he roasted as offerings to the gods. After destroying all evidence of what he had done, he returned home to his mother. He got into his cradle and acted like a helpless baby, but his mother knew that he had been up to no good. Apollo discovered the loss of his cattle and confronted Hermes, who sank down into his blankets with a look of childlike innocence. Apollo questioned the child about his stolen cattle, but Hermes claimed that he did not know anything; since he was born only yesterday, it was impossible that he could have committed such a crime. Apollo, however, was not fooled but knew Hermes for the sly-hearted cheat that he was.

The myth captures the enmity that obsessional Progressives feel toward the "antics" of Donald Trump. But the myth also hints at how the half-brothers represent two halves of a necessary whole—they are *shadow* figures for each other.

Humility

The obsessional is critical of himself and others. He may be self-deprecating and behave with humility, but this is due to covert feelings of grandiosity. The latter may be the most difficult element to access in the treatment of the obsessional. Firmly committed to appearing humble, the obsessional will adamantly deny any covert feelings of superiority to others. It is likely the flamboyant grandiosity of Donald Trump that most infuriates Progressive obsessionals.

Power and Control

Power is a key issue for obsessionals. Erich Fromm describes this in *Escape from Freedom*, in which he examines the *authoritarian personality*, which is essentially identical to the obsessional personality (Fromm, 1960). Fromm focuses primarily on the conflicts with respect to power and powerlessness that plague these individuals.

Returning now to the discussion of the authoritarian character, the most important feature to be mentioned is its attitude towards power. For the authoritarian character, there exist, so to speak, two sexes: the powerful ones and the powerless ones. His love, admiration, and readiness for submission are automatically aroused by power, whether of a person or an institution. Power fascinates him not for any values for which a specific power may stand, but just because it is power. Just as his "love" is automatically aroused by power, so powerless people or institutions automatically arouse his contempt. The very sight of a powerless person makes him want to attack, dominate, humiliate him.

> There is one feature of the authoritarian personality which has misled many observers: a tendency to defy authority and to resent any kind of influence from above…. Sometimes the attitude towards authority is divided. (Fromm, *Escape*, p. 167)

The developmental history of the obsessional often includes an authoritarian parent who made rigid demands on the child. Efforts at influencing the obsessional parent were unsuccessful, leaving the child frustrated and with a sense of powerlessness.

As an adult, the obsessional may be exquisitely attuned to power dynamics and compulsively seeks to gain control over others, so as not to relive childhood feelings of helplessness. If this cannot be achieved, passive-aggressive dynamics may emerge that covertly frustrate the power of others. Due to unexpressed feelings of early frustration, they can show an underlying destructiveness directed at the authoritarian parent. This can yield the impulse to destroy anything that reminds them of the authoritarian parental figure. Extreme Progressivism exhibits this underlying wish for destructiveness but often offers no viable alternative structure to replace it.

Perhaps no feature of the obsessional is more apparent to others than their need to control others. They insist on being in control in virtually all situations and become anxious and angry when the opportunity is denied them. As might be expected, the obsessional compulsively seeks positions of leadership and political influence. Only when exerting power over others do they feel immune to being controlled by them.

There is an optimal degree of personal space that individuals require for normal development, which varies between individuals. It may account for the misattuned interactions of some mothers and infants. Impingements develop through intrusions into both the psychological and physical domains of the child, and they are generally initiated by an anxious, controlling mother. The psychoanalyst Donald Winnicott suggests:

> Maternal failures produce phases of reaction to impingement and these reactions interrupt the 'going on being' of the infant. An excess of this reacting produces not frustration but a threat of annihilation. This in my view is a very real primitive anxiety, long antedating any anxiety that includes the word death in its description. (D Winnicott, 1966) p. 59)

Repeated impingements are experienced as traumatic, and when perceived as re-experienced by adults can trigger anxiety, anger, and despair.

The experience of the impinged upon child alternates between feeling overly scrutinized and ignored. The result is a profound sense of insecurity, a compulsive need to control self and others, and a deeply embedded conviction that others can be neither trusted nor of help. These adults may compulsively seek caretaking behaviors but ultimately reject them with a pseudo-independent aloofness. They represent "help-rejecting complainers" who invariably refuse to accept help when offered (R. Kradin, 2008).

Moral Masochism

One of the key elements for understanding the current positions adopted by obsessional Progressives is what Freud termed *moral masochism*. Freud recognized that there are individuals who derive a degree of unconscious pleasure from what would normally be viewed as pain. Masochism had been recognized prior to Freud's examination of the topic, but in *Ego and the Id* (Sigmund Freud, 1927) he introduced "what may be called a moral factor" to the topic. In his subsequent works, he examined the observation that certain individuals appeared to suffer "unconscious guilt" accompanied by a willingness to sustain abuse and self-defeating behaviors.

This position results from a confluence of motifs that include the obsessional's needs for perfectionism, guilt, and covert grandiosity. In general, the moral masochist views himself as powerless in the face of what he perceives to be a more powerful and abusive figure. But rather than admit defeat, he finds solace in believing that he is suffering for a higher moral cause. He chooses to sacrifice his conscious well-being for the subliminal pleasure of maintaining a morally superior self-image.

The myth of moral masochism appears in pagan religion and in Christianity. Prometheus, one of the Titans, was chained to a cliff for the crime of having given fire to man against the wishes of Zeus. Each day, his liver was eaten by an eagle; every night it regenerated. To end his torture, Prometheus needed only apologize to Zeus, but he refused, as he believed that his punishment was unjust. Instead, he chose to continue to suffer, as a communication of his moral superiority. The Christian myth has Jesus confronting powerful and unjust Roman and Temple authorities. He suffers and dies for the sins of man. Nietzsche recognized this as an example of moral masochism.

Several of the major issues promoted by Progressives fall into this category. Their unwillingness to acknowledge that radical Islam is the cause of world-wide terrorism and that allowing illegal alien criminals to remain in this country is a risk to law-abiding citizens are both examples of moral masochism. This leads us back to the question: What exactly is moral in today's America?

Chapter 7: Apocalyptic Psychology

I know not whether Laws be right or whether Laws be wrong...

—Oscar Wilde, *Ballad of Reading Gaol*

The extreme obsessional may be said to be suffering from apocalyptic psychology. The moral perfectionism, rigidity, striving for perception, anger and hostility, and persistent projections that may be seen in obsessionality all characterized those who have been members of apocalyptic sects. In recent years, the Branch Davidians, a sect of the Seventh Day Adventists, which came to a fiery end in Waco, Texas, embodied many of the features of an apocalyptic sect (Reavis, 1995). It is worthwhile to examine the features of apocalyptic thought to see how they parallel what is occurring in America today. Paul Hansen, a Harvard Professor of Religion, wrote in the 1970s (Hanson, 1979):

> To increasing numbers of observers it is becoming apparent that the dawn of a new apocalyptic era is upon us. Especially among those designated the "counter-culture" but not excluding many who continue overtly to live out their roles within the institutions of society, there is arising a profound disenchantment with the values and structures of our way of life. No longer does the optimism go unquestioned that ample education and hard work will be rewarded with all the benefits of the good life. At the heart of the matter is the collapse of confidence in the god to which twentieth-century Western man faithfully dedicated life and soul. Progress—a being infused with life by technology's discoveries and worshipped in anticipation of unlimited material return. (Hansen, p. 1)

This prescient statement suggests that the rise of apocalyptic psychology has been recognized for almost the last half-century.

Apocalyptic thought in ancient Judaism emerged in the period between the end of the "Old Testament" and the appearance of the "New," a period of several hundred years. In his *History of the Jews*, Josephus in the first century CE described four distinct "philosophies" that were prevalent in the time of the Second Temple. One was that of the Essenes, whom he described as leading a monastic life of purity. Virtually nothing more was known about the Essenes until modern times, although they were noted by Greek historian Pliny the Elder in his *Natural Histories* to have lived near the Dead Sea close to the village of Ein Gedi.

In 1947, an Arab shepherd discovered a cache of scrolls in the caves of the Judean desert at Qumran. These included the writings dating back to no later than the first century CE. Some of the scrolls described an ascetic community living apart from other Jews under rigorous conditions. The sectarian literature exhibited an ideology based on radical dualistic thinking and spoke of a great struggle, pitting forces of Light against those of Darkness. The sect at its beginnings was apparently led by a High Priest of Righteousness who was deposed by a Wicked Priest. The sect describes itself as being persecuted by the authorities. It expresses contempt for what it perceived as the corruption and impurity of the Second Temple establishment. But they imagined that at the end of times, they would regain control of the Temple, and their enemies would be destroyed. Archeological evidence at Qumran suggests that its inhabitants disappeared abruptly and were likely destroyed by the Romans in the War against the Jews (66-73 CE).

The sect had rituals that were both rigid and severe. They called for a degree of greater ritual purity than those practiced by their Jewish contemporaries. Like the early Christians, they practiced extensive baptismal rites. All monies and goods were shared by the community, and infractions of its rules resulted in punishment and expulsion from the community. The sect referred to itself as "The Way," which curiously was also a term by which the earliest Christian community designated itself. Although scholarly efforts to link the Jesus movement to this sect have largely been rejected, there is some question as to whether John the Baptist may have been a member (G Vermes, 2004).

The Dead Sea sect differed with their fellow Jews on questions of morality and ritual purity. Members of the sect were certain that their ideas constituted God's will and, therefore, the highest good. They exhibited an obvious hatred of those who did not share their views. This story sounds familiar.

Like the Dead Sea sect, Progressive and Conservative obsessionals are unable to agree or compromise on their moral "ideals." But only periodically in American history have such extreme views divided the country like they do today. America's moral values as a society were traditionally liberal Enlightenment ones. Tolerance generally held sway over extremism. America strived toward achieving a proper balance between the extremes of unbounded Christian love and excessive Judaic strictness. The philosopher Jurgan Habermas emphasizes (Habermas, 1981; Habermas & Ratzinger, 2006):

> Universalistic egalitarianism, from which spring the ideals of freedom and a collective life in solidarity, the autonomous conduct of life and emancipation, the individual morality of conscience, human rights, and democracy, is the direct legacy of the Judaic ethic of justice and the Christian ethic of love. (Habermas, *Dialects*, p. 11)

David Gelernter argues that the Puritan founders of America derived meaning in comparing themselves with the ancient Israelites entering the Promised Land (Gerlernter, 2007). In addition to their Christian emphasis on love of their fellow man, they revered Judaism's ethic of law. They saw the virtue in law, as a path toward diminished narcissistic preoccupation. The ancient Judaic emphasis on values, family, and kinship were dear to them.

In contrast, Christianity is a melding of Judaic morality with Hellenistic[26] philosophy. The sociologist Robert Nisbet states, "The Greeks

---

26 Hellenism refers to the philosophy spread throughout much of the known world beginning in the fourth century BCE in the wake of Alexander the Great's conquests. Alexander, having been mentored by Aristotle, envisioned a world universally immersed

above any people known to us in antiquity, were fascinated by change, its sources, properties, directions, and its relation to the principles of organic growth" (Nisbet, 1969) p. 3). Progress and rationality were the goals of Hellenism, and unlike Judaism, it fostered a universalist ethic that largely ignored ancient religious distinctions and ethnicities. These ideas were adopted by early Pauline Christianity. As Paul argues in Galatians 3:28, "There is neither Jew nor Gentile, neither slave nor free, nor is there male and female, for you are all one in Christ Jesus."

As a reform movement within first-century CE Judaism attempting to attract pagan converts, Paul decided to break with Judaic Law, which was viewed by pagans as overly burdensome. To attract concerts, Paul imagined a new faith, one based on forgiveness of sin via the belief in salvific death and resurrection of Christ. This move toward anomia (i.e., a reduced emphasis on law) is evidenced by Paul's argument in Romans 7:

> It was the law that showed me my sin. I would never have known that coveting is wrong if the law had not said, "You must not covet." But sin used this command to arouse all kinds of covetous desires within me! If there were no law, sin would not have that power. At one time, I lived without understanding the law. But when I learned the command not to covet, for instance, the power of sin came to life, and I died. So, I discovered that the law's commands, which were supposed to bring life, brought spiritual death instead.

Indeed, as historian of religion Gershom Scholem suggests, messianism in any faith is virtually always accompanied by anomic impulses. However, law is subsequently reemphasized when the expected end time does not materialize (Scholem, 1995). Even Paul, who unquestionably believed that he was living at the end of times, found it necessary to modify his message to the early Christian community in Corinth when he learned that they had been ignoring the rules of society before the arrival of the end time. In brief, the earliest forms of Christianity preached the primacy of the spirit and viewed the law as an unwelcome constraint.

---

in Greek language and philosophy.

When the end time did not materialize and as Christianity spread and became increasingly institutionalized within the Roman Empire, its early anomic impulses faded and were replaced by detailed Canon Law. By the sixteenth century, Martin Luther, a young German Augustinian monk, like Paul, also found himself plagued with guilt and concerns for his own salvation. In the psychobiography *Young Man Luther*, the psychoanalyst Erik Erikson describes Luther as a classical obsessional neurotic (Erikson, 1995). Like Paul, he chose to assuage his own guilty conscience by reestablishing the notion of *faith* as the source of salvation, eliminating the need for the prescribed *works* of Roman Catholicism that were rooted in Christianity's Judaic heritage.

Protestant Reform

As Protestantism evolved, interest in reading the "Old Testament" was rekindled. Old Testament figures—Abraham, Isaac, Jacob, Moses, and David—became role models for the faithful, and lawful society again an increasingly important basis of the Protestant vision. The strong belief in predestination in Calvinism fostered a new intense work ethic, which, as the philosopher Max Weber suggested, laid the foundations for capitalism, the nation state, scientific exploration, secularism, and in due course, for America as well (Weber, 2002).

Obsessional Guilt

Until recently, obsessional guilt was attributable to an individual's perceived transgressions of the Judeo-Christian ethic. But since the 1960s, Progressivism in America has fostered a new version of anomia, one that, like early Christianity, has been increasingly focused on social justice issues and antagonistic to the rule of law. Progressives perceive themselves as compassionate defenders of the disenfranchised.

However, current Progressive perceptions of what constitutes disenfranchisement are viewed by others as extreme. For example, in America there are increasing numbers of educated middle class and well-to-do blacks, as well as women and Hispanics serving at the heights of the U.S. government. Since the 1960s, white America has opened its doors to women and people of color. There is less overt prejudice than ever before—less than virtually anywhere else in the world, including Africa. But these facts are judged by Progressives as imperfect so that they can persist in claiming that America is a "racist" nation (Horowitz, 2016).

The obsessional experiences guilt for his imperfections. But the world is not, and likely never will be, perfect. But what they are doing is projecting their own sense of "victimhood" onto others. This can at times be traced to their fears of abandonment.

A 48-year-old obsessional woman was the mother of a young boy with a modest but nondebilitating physical disability. She would present dreams where both she and a child were under attack from evil apocalyptic forces. In these dreams, it was her role to protect the child. Her own childhood had been harsh, and she was both mentally and physically neglected.

Her dream includes an archetypal image of a mother protecting her child. It was described two thousand years ago by the author of the New Testament's apocalyptic Book of Revelation, as Mary protecting the baby Jesus from the chaos that surrounded them. But lest this be interpreted as a dynamic limited to mothers, I know of fathers today who worry excessively about the welfare of their children, hovering about to make certain that they are perfectly protected.

It is not surprising that obsessional Progressives feel that they have a moral duty not to be bigoted, not to be racist, not to judge anyone for their gender—indeed, not to judge anyone at all. To be so would imply that they were critical and unkind. But what they deny is that they are covertly critical most of the time. The superego of the obsessional judges imperfections and failures harshly. Their judgments occur for the most part either outside of their awareness or tend to be guised, lest they risk displaying their hostility to others. Their targets extend to the disenfranchised groups that they openly assiduously defend, as in reality they tend to view them as weak, which is something they criticize themselves for. Overt criticism and hostilities are generally expressed at a safe distance and toward those who do not share their value, and who they consequently see as repugnant. It is not uncommon in psychotherapy to hear a patient describe how he or she confronted an individual in an angry way, only to discover upon probing that this was instead a fantasy and not a real event.

One Law for the Haves and Have Nots

One of the ethical advances of Judaism was a code of laws that expresses concerns for widows, orphans, the poor, and aliens. The ancient Israelites were cautioned remember that they were once "strangers in a strange land" and slaves in Egypt, and to not take advantage of or treat these particular groups harshly.[27] Ancient Israelite law called for measured and humane modes of punishment for legal infractions, as compared to literal interpretations of an "eye for an eye" seen in the punishments actually called for in the legal codes of the ancient Near East.[28] The Prophetic tradition of social justice, especially the Book of Isaiah, formed the basis for Jesus' teachings and those of the early Church.[29] But the teachings of Jesus were extreme with respect to those of most of the other sects of Second Temple Judaism, except the Dead Sea sect. In his Sermon on the

---

27   The "Law" as used here and referred to in the New Testament is the Hebrew *Torah*, which is derived from a Hebrew root, *hrh,* that means "instruction." The *Torah* includes the five books of Moses. The entire Jewish Law, which may not have been practiced in the first century CE, includes the Oral Law and 613 Commandments, 365 proscriptions, and 248 positive commandments. Because many pertained to the Temple cult, the current number is far smaller, although they are all considered topics for study in Rabbinic Judaism.

28   Despite biblical phrases that call for punishments that include an "eye for an eye, a tooth for a tooth," etc., the law has been consistently interpreted since antiquity as requiring monetary payments rather than physical body parts in civil cases. The driving idea is that the punishment should fit the crime and not be barbaric and extreme.

29   There are multiple references in the Gospels to the Hebrew prophets and in particular to the Book of Isaiah.

Mount, Jesus suggests that one is as culpable for sinful thoughts as for sinful acts, thus holding man to a perfectionist morality that had not previously characterized Judaism. But this must be interpreted as an example of apocalyptic psychology. Jesus believed that the end time and the advent of the *Kingdom of God* was nigh, and that event would perfect man. To prepare for this, striving for moral perfectionism was necessary. But the end did not come, at least not in recognizable terms.

As the philosopher Frederic Nietzsche noted, Christianity extols perfectionistic morality, which in his opinion serves to undermine the well-being of a society (Nietsche, 2017). As he suggested in a pre-psychoanalytical world:

In helpful and benevolent people one nearly always finds a clumsy cunning that first rearranges the person who is to be helped so that, for example, he "deserves" their help, needs their help and will prove to be deeply grateful, dependent, subservient for all their help. With fantasies such as these they control the needy like a piece of property.... (Nietzsche, *On Genealogy*, p. 194)

Nietzsche's opinion parallels that of Conservative detractors of Progressivism who argue that they choose to foster dependency and undermine human potential, thereby promoting a permanent "underclass." This is the basis of the political conflicts concerning who should be allowed to remain on welfare and immigrate to America.

An example of such an impractical high moral standard when applied politically in a hostile world occurred on the Indian subcontinent under the rule of *Ashoka*, king of the Indian Maurya Dynasty in the third century BCE. This Vedic warlord underwent a personal transformation, ostensibly due to guilt for the bloodshed in his military campaigns. He experienced an epiphany and adopted the peaceful and compassionate tenets of Buddhism for his kingdom.[30] Various stele monuments were erected by

---

30 Those who study comparative religion, including Joseph Campbell, have envisioned Buddhism as an effort to escape from the present world, and therefore is not a pragmatic theosophy to apply to pragmatic daily life. In Buddhism, a professional group of mo-

Ashoka and are extant. They laud the virtues of peaceful coexistence and an abhorrence of anger and violence. Yet following his death, Ashoka's kingdom reverted to its original warlike ways to protect itself from the hostilities of its non-Buddhist neighbors.

The English writer H.G. Wells wrote in his *Outline of History*: "Amidst the tens of thousands of names of monarchs that crowd the columns of history, their majesties and graciousnesses, and serenities and royal high-nesses and the like, the name of Ashoka shines, and shines, almost alone, a star" (Wells, 2004) p. 394). But Wells was clear that unilateral pacifism in a hostile world was fraught with danger.

In *Time Machine*, penned at the turn of the *fin di siècle*, he imagined a future when humanity would be divided into two groups; the *Eloi*, who were highly morally evolved but no longer capable of protecting them-selves, and the *Morlocks*, a primitive hostile group that preyed upon the defenseless *Eloi* at will (Wells, 2016). This is the risk that America as-sumes in adopting Progressive pacifist ideas in a world that remains dan-gerous. Failing to recognize this truth is potentially irreversibly self-de-feating, and must be judged as wrong-headed in practice.

What in fact protects individuals and nations, as America's Founding Fathers recognized, is not the well-intentioned charity or compassion of others, but the rule of law and the ability to defend against those who seek to do harm. Charity and compassion are too often tainted by misguided motivations to be an effective guiding principle for government.

Freud noted in *Mourning and Melancholia* that obsessionals are prone to self-defeating and masochistic behaviors. (S Freud, 1959b) What is at issue is how can one differentiate noble virtues from obsessional psycho-pathology? The simple answer is that it cannot be done, especially at the collective level. As noble ideas can be misguided, one must optimally encourage policies of peace supported by strength

---

nastics practice meditative Buddhism, whereas the rest of the community gains merit by supporting them.

Whereas the Hebrew Bible insists that one must not mistreat the disadvantaged, it sets out specific rules as to how this should be done. Charity is to be given to the poor with regularity. In the ancient agricultural society, the corners of one's fields and vineyards were to be left for the poor to glean from. But it also warns that the disadvantaged are not exempt from the rules of society, rather they must be treated no better nor worse than the wealthy and influential. As it says in Leviticus 11:27, "You shall do no unrighteousness in judgement; you shall *not* respect the honor of the poor, nor honor the person of the mighty; but in righteousness you shall judge your neighbor." There are no provisions that suggest that individuals or society should place themselves at a disadvantage to achieve social or economic equality or to assuage unwarranted feelings of guilt. But in this regard, Judaism differs from the precepts of early Christianity, which counsels in Mark that It is "easier for a camel to go through the eye of a needle, and to "turn the other cheek" to those who have done you harm.

Golden Rule

The standard of the Judeo-Christian ethic is often distilled to the "Golden Rule." Judaism phrases the "Golden Rule" differently than Jesus does in the Gospels. The Judaic form of the Rule is apodictic, i.e., "Do *not* do unto others what you do *not* want done to yourself," as opposed to Jesus' dictum, "Do unto others what you want done to yourself." The former emphasizes protecting the individual rather than imposing self-determined ideas of what may be "good" for others. Many in the Inquisitions suffered and died from the consequences of well-intentioned Christian love, and some, like the family of Kate Steinle,[31] have suffered in America from comparable ideas expressed by Progressivism.

The *Golden Rule* has been critically examined by scholars. According

---

31 This young woman was killed by a gun that discharged in the hand of a several-time deported illegal alien from Mexico. The case became a cause for Conservative arguments against amnesty for criminal illegal aliens. When the case was eventually tried in the sanctuary city of San Francisco, the killer was acquitted of murder or manslaughter and was referred for possible charges of illegal possession of a deadly weapon.

to the philosopher Marcus Singer in the *Golden Rule* (Neusner & Chilton, 2009), "The nearly universal acceptance of the golden rule and its promulgation by persons of considerable intelligence, though otherwise of divergent outlooks, would…seem to provide some evidence for the claim that it is a universal ethical truth" (Neusner, *Golden*; p. 2). But the ethicist Bernard Gert in the same text avers:

> The golden Rule is not really a very good rule of conduct. . . . If followed literally, and how else are we to understand it, it requires all normal policemen not to arrest criminals, and all normal judges not to sentence them. . . . The Golden Rule also requires, and students might like this, that teachers not give flunking grades to students even if they deserve it. (Neusner, *Golden,* p. 3)

Indeed, there are many Americans who agree with Gert's concerns about the *Golden Rule*.

Sigmund Freud expressed little enthusiasm for the *Golden Rule*, which he examined in *Civilization and its Discontents* (S Freud, 1930). He viewed it as psychologically unrealistic, because it requires the repression of the instinctive basis of love. It devalues love by failing to discriminate between those one feels genuine affection for and those one does not. Freud strongly disagreed with Jesus argument of "turning the other cheek." He saw it as unjust, as the character of man is flawed. According to Freud:

> Civilization pays no attention to all this; it merely admonishes us that the harder it is to obey the precept, the more meritorious it is to do so. But anyone who follows such a precept in present-day civilization only puts himself at a disadvantage vis-a vis the person who disregards it. (Freud, *Civilization*, p. 143)

Freud was not a proponent of religion, and he viewed the Christian version of the *Golden Rule* as "other worldly." He wrote, "At this point, the ethics based on religion introduces its promises of a better after life. But so long as virtue is not rewarded here on earth, ethics will, I fancy, preach in vain" (Neusner & Chilton, 2009) p. 87).

Phillip Rieff argues in *Freud the Mind of the Moralist* that Freud expected psychoanalysis would eventually replace religion as society's basis of morality (Rieff, 1979). However, he was reticent to admit that his "science" of psychoanalysis was not truly novel but instead was in large measure simply a reworking of Judaic morality. But he would undoubtedly not have been pleased to see his ideas used to transform society into a "culture of therapy" driven by pervasive notions of psychological trauma and victimization. Even in his earliest theorizing, Freud withdrew his early "trauma theory," not to protect the fathers of Vienna from accusation of father-daughter incest, but because he realized that if one defined "trauma" loosely, everyone would be victimized. Individual responsibility was the key to Freud's mature psychology, much as it is in Judaism (R. Kradin, 2016).

Kant and the Unconstrained Vision

Contrast Freud's pessimistic "realism" with the ideas of the eighteenth century German Christian philosopher Immanuel Kant (Kant, 1780). Kant conceived of a moral *categorical imperative* based on pure reason, one detached from feelings—a typical obsessional idea—in which man is compelled to adopt the highest moral stance regardless of reciprocity or the presence or absence of the desire of others to be treated as such. For Kant, abstract morality was the highest virtue. All men are required to behave rationally and honestly regardless of the effect that it might have on others, even if it is deleterious. Kant's idealistic perspective is at odds with Freud's pragmatism.

But as Rieff notes, the concept of responsible morality is currently being eroded by the therapeutic mindset of liberal Progressivism. Immoral behaviors are increasingly considered the result of psychopathology that requires therapy, rather than punitive action (Rieff, 1966). According to Rieff, it is assumed in Progressive society that all disadvantaged individuals have been victims of adverse socioeconomic conditions, developmental abuse, or societal racism and bigotry. Violent criminals, they argue, are suffering the complications of harsh treatment or deprivation. Furthermore, virtually all physical and mental disadvantages are termed "disabilities." Consequently, individuals are not encouraged to take responsibility for their actions, and their moral failings are not held against them. Yet many have grown up under difficult circumstances, even or are seriously physically impaired, and have become law abiding productive members of society. Generic labelling is overly simplistic.

For example, the "poor" are in fact a heterogeneous group that includes those who are economically challenged because they are truly disabled, or lack the skills required to perform productive work. But there are others who lack motivation and prefer being supported by others, as well as those who make every effort to better their situation but for lack of luck are not successful at overcoming their economic disadvantages. For Progressives, these distinctions hardly seem to matter. Instead all are considered equally disadvantaged and in need of government assistance.

Steven Sondheim's lyrics in the tune "Officer Krupke" in the 1957 American urban adaptation of Shakespeare's *Romeo and Juliet, West Side Story,* captures the opposing perspectives of Conservatives and Progressives on culpability. In the song's lyrics, a juvenile delinquent is shuffled back and forth between the police, magistrates, psychiatrists, and social workers, without any clarity as to who has the authority to rule on his fate. In Progressive America, negation has been all but abrogated and replaced by enablement and gratification in an ill-conceived effort at preserving self-esteem, rather than recognizing that genuine self-esteem derives from taking personal responsibility, and this includes experiencing honest regret, guilt, shame, culpability, punishment, and atonement. This is the only moral stance that ultimately improves a society. Producing a welfare "underclass" has never been demonstrated to improve a society.

The "Old Testament" considers the balance of love and fear (awe) of God to be the ultimate compass for morality. The sixteenth century Kabbalah theosophy and its subsequent adaptation by Hassidism as a personal psychology, emphasizes the balance of "love" (*chesed*) and "limitation" (*gevurah*). Whereas evil is imagined as deriving from excessive harsh-ness, unbounded love is equally problematic. The co-expression of both "Good" and "Evil" within the Godhead is an essential requirement of pure monotheism, which differs in this regard from all dualistic religions. As Isaiah 45:7 states, "I am the Lord, I create good *and* evil." Religions, including Christianity, that ascribe "Good" to God, as the fourth century CE Church Father Augustine did as the *summum bonum,* and "Evil" to a Satanic counterpart, are in fact expressing a non-monotheistic theology. In this regard, it is noteworthy that Augustine had been a follower of the radically dualistic sect of Manicheanism before being baptized into ortho-dox Christianity.

But even modern psychologists like Jung have questioned the concept of God as all "good," at least in man's terms. He argued that such radical splitting of good and evil has limiting effects on the human psyche and contributes the development of a "shadow" (i.e., repressed contents that might otherwise be acceptable to consciousness). When what is "bad" includes all that is not perfectly "good," the circumstances are set for massive projections.

Like an apocalyptic ideology, the obsessional psyche is structured as a radical duality. Good and evil are experienced in black and white terms; there is little room for grey. They believe that they are aligned with the "Good," as they "Evil" is repressed and projected onto others. This is a metastable and dangerous psychological dynamic, because it fosters hos-tile and at times violent reactions toward those holding opposing views. The fact is that there is a "religious war" transpiring in America today, and it may ultimately prove as destructive as other historical conflicts have. But instead of one religious sect opposing another, it is being fought by those holding opposing "secular" visions of the highest "Good."

A secular society, motivated by unconstrained "love" and willing to forego the rule of law, errs by "throwing out the baby with the bath water," and potentially sets the stage for the unraveling of a society. Like in indi-vidual psychology, boundaries and limit setting are necessary for normal development. The unopposed gratification of a child, does not lead, as some have erroneously concluded in their idealism, to adults with improved self-esteem, rather it results in a child and eventually an adult that is narcissistic entitled with a precarious sense of self-worth. Discipline and discernment are necessary to achieve a mature sense of self and an internal moral compass. Whereas "Love," as Paul suggests in 1Corinthians, may be the highest ethical aspiration, it is meaningless unless one can distinguish it from artefact, and there is no "Archimedean point" that allows one to do that with certainty. The notion at times promoted by Progressive psychotherapists that "healing" occurs via "unconditional love" is a fantasy but one with broad appeal for those who lack the courage to bear responsibility for their own behaviors. The results of such approaches have a predictable way of backfiring. As one of my psychoanalytical supervisors warned, "No good deed goes unpunished." Or as an anonymous proverb suggests, "The road to hell is paved with good intentions."

The Rabbinic sages were primarily concerned with morality and purity laws that were particular to Jews, but they did not ignore the moral obligations of the non-Jewish world. The so-called seven Noachide laws were judged to be the minimal requirements for establishing a stable society. These include the expected prohibitions of not killing or stealing but also extend to the forbidding of cruelty to animals. But the last law is crucial, although somewhat unexpected. The seventh Noachide law calls on non-Jews to create a system of courts to legislate and enforce society's law. Disrespect for a ruling government, even a tyrannical one, was viewed as fundamentally immoral. In Chapter 3:2 of the Talmudic tractate *Ethics of the Fathers*, Rabbi Chanina, deputy to the Priests, suggests: "Pray for the integrity of the government; for were it not for the fear of its authority, a man would swallow his neighbor alive" (Lau, 2007). Despite Roman antipathy toward the Jews at that time, the Rabbinic sages realized that laws were essential for preserving a society. It is also evident that this attitude was incorporated into Freud's view of mankind.

But in America today, there is a disturbing perspective on the part of some Progressives that the rule of law is optional if it conflicts with their ideas concerning moral "progress." But secular humanism has never been demonstrated to include a morality that was not ultimately rooted in the Judeo-Christian ethic (Habermas & Ratzinger, 2006). The question is whether one chooses to adopt a pragmatic morality with elements of responsibility and law, or a utopian morality that has never been successful in *this* world. If there is doubt concerning this fact, one only need examine the abundant statistically significant *facts* that demonstrate the trends in poverty and crime in the inner cities, the widespread deterioration of performance on educational testing, and the lack of civility on university campuses since the 1960s, when the liberal Progressive agenda was instituted (C Murray, 1984).

Post-modernist ideas of morality suggest that it is a relative construct with agreed-upon standards. By their argument, one is entitled to invent one's own morality, and no one has a legitimate right to question them. But this is an untenable definition, and it makes constructive dialogue impossible.

Science of Morality

In *A Natural History of Morality*, Michael Tomasello suggests that morality emerged from a mammalian drive for interdependence (Tomasello, 2016). As Tomasello notes:

> The first (level of cooperation) is simply the cooperative proclivities of great apes in general, organized around a special sympathy for kin and friends: the first person I save from a burning shelter is my child or spouse, no deliberation needed. The second is a joint morality of collaboration in which I have specific responsibilities to specific individuals in specific circumstances: the next person I save is the firefighting partner with whom I am currently collaborating (and with whom I have a joint commitment) to extinguish the fire. The third is a more impersonal collective morality of cultural norms and institutions in which all members of the cultural group are equally valuable. . . . The coexistence of these different moralities . . . is of course anything but peaceful. (Tomasello, *Natural History*, p. 15)

In recent years, efforts have also been directed at "quantifying" differences in morality between Conservatives and Progressives. The New York University psychologist, Jonathan Haidt (2012) describes the responses to a Moral Foundations Questionnaire, which was scored with the political positions held by the subjects. The test included subscales hypothesized to contribute to the moral stance of the subjects. These included (1) caring for others, (2) fairness, (3) loyalty, (4) respect for authority, and (5) ideas concerning sanctity.

What Haidt—himself a self-professed liberal—discovered was that "liberal" subjects scored high with respect to caring for others and for fairness, but low with respect to other parameters. The "conservative" subjects also scored high with respect to care and fairness, but additionally scored high with respect to concerns for loyalty, respect for authority, and the idea of what is sacred. Haidt concluded that Conservative morality was not different, but more "complex," than that of liberals.

Additional studies of subject reactions were measured by electroencephalogram (EEG) traces. These demonstrated that "Liberal" brains reacted more strongly to phrases that rejected care for others and fairness concerns (e.g., "Total equality at the workplace is unrealistic") than did "Conservatives." As Haidt argues, the political positions that people express are not based primarily on reason, but on preexisting emotional reactions. Rationales justifying their feelings follow secondarily, a phenomenon referred to as "confirmation bias." When core values were questioned in these studies, subjects tended to either change the subject or to cast blame on others.

Presumably with the aim of promoting dialogue, Haidt describes attempting to convey his findings to Democratic voters. He informed them that based on his findings, their claims that Conservatives are "mean-spirited" or psychological distorted were incorrect. Rather, he suggested, most Conservatives are both sincere and well-intentioned. Their moral positions are, according to Haidt, more nuanced and fact-based than those of Progressive liberals.

As Gelernter notes, the American creed is based on decency and re-spect for the differences of its citizenry (Gerlernter, 2007). Despite their many different countries of origin and religious and cultural ties, Ameri-cans share a kinship bond with each other. This has been based on a shared sense of moral values. History does not support the view that America is a racist, bigoted, war-mongering, abusive nation that some extreme Pro-gressives have suggested. America has not been perfect; but all things considered, history instead demonstrates that it has done more to foster liberty and human rights in the world than any other nation in history. This should lead to national pride that reinforces moral bonds, yet there are currently increasingly vocal Americans who profess hatred for this country. "Love it, or leave it!" is not the answer. But critically questioning the basis for strong negative views based on a paucity of carefully cher-ry-picked evidence is justified.

David Horowitz argues in *Unholy Alliance* that some Progressives exhibit greater sympathy for Islamic terrorists than they do for Ameri-can victims of terror. The Reverend Jeremiah Wright, the spiritual leader of the Trinity United Church of Christ that Barack Obama attended for many years in Chicago,[32] remarked following the American tragedy of 9/11/2001 that "terrorism begets terrorism," and quoted the Black Mus-lim leader Elijah Muhammed, proclaiming that "America's chickens were coming home to roost." Rather than "God bless America, it should be God Damn America," preached Wright from the pulpit. Such stances run counter to the natural bond of kinship in society, which as Tomasello ar-gues, is a core, and likely hard-wired, feature of morality.

Deep-seated hostilities can crystallize around disparate moral stanc-

---

32 One of the extraordinary facts of the 2008 presidential election was that Barack Obama, a veritable unknown on the national stage, was elected president with virtually no critical vetting. His relationship to the Reverend Wright, terrorists, and other mem-bers of the radical left might have given most Americans pause. But the liberal Progres-sive press failed to explore these facts in depth, apparently charmed by the notion of having the first African American president. They adopted the same attitude to Obama throughout his two terms; he was rarely held seriously responsible for a series of fiascos and untruths.

es. This is well-known from the history of religion. Religionists tend to develop affiliative bonds with those who share their moral views, the so-called "in-group." An in-group may exhibit limited tolerance for some others the group if their values are not too disparate. For example, as an Abrahamic monotheistic religion, Islam shares history and certain values with both Judaism and Christianity, that it does not with pagan religions (e.g., Buddhism[33] or Hinduism).

For centuries after the rise and spread of Islam, Jews and Christians living in the Islamic world were accepted as underclass minorities. They were tolerated but often ill-treated and forced to pay a special underclass *dhimmi* tax. On the other hand, pagans had the choice of either converting to Islam or dying by the sword. But even this minimal degree of tolerance is no longer seen in countries that observe fundamentalist forms of Islam. It is not possible for Jews or Christians to live in Saudi Arabia. In addition, Islamic anti-Semitism has increased dramatically since the founding of the state of Israel, as its very existence is viewed by many Muslims as an affront to Islam.

There are few to no Jews currently living in Islamic countries that had been their home for centuries, including Iraq, Yemen, and Libya. Coptic Christians are regularly murdered in Egypt, and the Christian populations of Lebanon and Syria live daily with the fear of pogroms (Horowitz, 2004). Yet these situations seem to evoke little criticism by Progressives, who believe that to acknowledge the truth of these injustices would stigmatize Muslims and promote Conservative "narratives." Morality may be many things, but it is certainly not supposed to be hypocritical or convenient.

---

33 The destruction of priceless ancient Buddhist statuary in Bamiyan by the Taliban is an example of how fundamentalist Islamists view paganism. Buddhism is an a-theistic tradition derived from pagan Hinduism, and therefore falls well beyond the pale for Islam

Who We Are

Progressivism was conceived as an ideology with Christian values. But in recent years, it has adopted a secularized and radical interpretation of Christian social justice. The Progressive agenda is currently focused on feminism, identity politics, and socioeconomic disparities, virtually to the exclusion of all other issues. In *Who We Are,* the late Harvard professor Samuel Huntington argued that America's exceptional success on the world stage was primarily attributable to the values and efforts of the white European Protestants who founded the American colonies (Huntington, 2005). Prior to the 1960s, America absorbed millions of immigrants from all over the world—those who were willing to adopt core American values and speak English. Since 1965, large-scale immigrations from Central America, Asia, the Middle East, and Africa have brought new cultures to these shores, some largely unacquainted with, and in some cases not desirous of, adopting America's values. Huntington warned that if the assimilation of new immigrants was unsuccessful, America's values and its "exceptionalism" could be compromised in the future.

Although viewed as politically incorrect and met with hostility by Progressives, Huntington's ideas cannot *a priori* be labeled as racist or bigoted, because they have been confirmed by scientific studies (C Murray, 1984). Some—although certainly not all—Hispanics who come to this country *illegally* lack the educational preparation necessary to foster success in American society. Some are functionally illiterate and unable to read, write, or speak even the minimal amounts of English required to gain employment. In addition, entering a country illegally does not necessarily bode well for future law-abiding behavior. At the current time, illegal entrance into America means that these immigrants have no future path toward citizenship, although in many states they will qualify for the benefits of entitlement programs.

The Founding Fathers were aware that the success of a democratic Republic requires a certain level of civic knowledge concerning its values and workings. It is questionable whether immigrants, or even native-born citizens, who have been minimally educated can sustain a democracy (D'Souza, 1991). In *The Bell Curve* (Herrnstein & Murray, 1994), a controversial text but one supported by numerous statistically significant facts, the authors reported that the *mean* intelligence quotient (IQ) of African blacks and Mexican Hispanics was well below that of immigrants of European descent.

Their findings should not be—and were not—interpreted to suggest that peoples of color are intellectually inferior, but they should raise concerns that there may be differences in intelligence that cannot be dismissed solely on the bases of ethnic, cultural, or socioeconomic backgrounds. Asians who have immigrated to America from very different cultures than our own routinely score high on these standardized tests, and as a group tend to rival or surpass native-born Americans or immigrants from Western Europe, with respect to academic achievement. The interpretations of facts should be encouraged; denying them should be condemned as nonprogressive.

However, the results of these studies do suggest that the usual Progressive solutions to this problem are unlikely to be effective, and history has now demonstrated that they have not been (D'Souza, 1991). There is currently no scientific evidence that entitlement programs or government-driven educational programs that cater to poor school performance have led to any significant improvement in the IQ scores or academic performance of African-Americans as a group. Other potentially explanatory factors, such as high divorce rate, the absence of two parents in a household, and poor attitudes toward academic success are realities in many urban neighborhoods inhabited by people of color (C Murray, 1999). But these are not addressed by Progressives who view the traditional family structures as "overrated" and as an affront to the potential of single women or homosexual couples to optimally raise children. They turn a blind eye to important facts and instead persist in arguing that government must support society's failures by providing economic supports.

As IQ is demonstrably the most accurate indicator of future socioeconomic success in American society, *The Bell Jar's* findings should be a concern for *all* citizens. They raise concern for whether America is likely to benefit from policies that include indiscriminate immigration through "open borders" (Herrnstein & Murray, 1994). If Progressives continue to avoid these issues because they are perceived as "cruel," "heartless," "bigoted" or "racist," there is no possibility of arriving at real political solutions. Progressives used to consider themselves "scientific." If this is the case, then they should be asked to provide *credible* evidence to support their policies.

Immigrants here *illegally* and unable to speak English must live in closed ethnic communities to survive. Had they immigrated legally, they would have received the necessary education to foster citizenship. But without that education, they are likely to remain on the welfare rolls of the state or in low-paying jobs, or worse, have to resort to criminal activities to support themselves. The frequently heard argument that illegal immigrants are "willing to do the jobs that American citizens won't do" is both incorrect and frankly degrading. It suggests that Americans are willing to create a permanent underclass to serve their needs. Consider the following definition of *slave* in the *Oxford English Dictionary:* "A person who works very hard without proper remuneration or appreciation." How many Progressives would actively defend slavery in America.

The Specific Problem with Islam

Unfortunately, the world is experiencing an outbreak of fundamental Islamic terrorism, directed in part at America. Some, but certainly not all, immigrants from the Islamic world do not approve of America's secularism. Their interpretation of Islam disapproves of feminism, gay rights, etc. These Muslims choose to live in ethnic neighborhoods, where they are confronted daily with having to choose between the values of their newly adopted country and their allegiance to the orthodoxies of their faith. Muslims who embrace American values are rarely fundamentalists.

Comparable conflicts between secular and traditional religious values are not new. However, they have not been problematic for all faiths, and this is best explained by aggressive theocratic underpinnings of Islam that can be found in the Quran and that are still practiced in fundamentalist Muslim countries, like Wahabi Saudi Arabia.

Fundamentalist Muslims have every right, and perhaps even good reason, for not approving of American culture today. There are other religious groups, including ultra-Orthodox Jews, Christian Amish, and some Mormons, who also choose to live apart from mainstream secular society in America. But these groups have not perpetrated terrorist attacks aimed at killing Americans.

The concept of *jihad,* or struggle, has two distinct meanings in Islam. It can be used to refer to an individual struggle against moral imperfection or as a political struggle against those in the non-Islamic world. Progressives are either ignorant of or actively choose to deny this, although it has been a core aspect of orthodox Islam since its inception. Most Muslims in America do not adhere to fundamentalist interpretations of Islam religion. But loyalty to their co-religionists may explain why condemnation of fundamentalist terrorism by Muslim clerics in America has been faint.

Too many naïve Americans cannot fathom the notion that there are people in the world who do not like them and mean them harm. Progressives maintain an optimistic stance that terrorism will end if we treat Islamic fundamentalists "kindly" and allow them to learn more about the good intentions of Americans. Or consider the groundless argument that terrorists are disenfranchised young Muslim men who would reject terrorism if they only had better-paying jobs. The truth has nothing to do with any of these arguments. All reports indicate that fundamentalist Islamic terrorists have *no* desire to adopt the secular values of the West. There is no reason to conclude that they are hoping to get rich and successful in America; they will not respond to being treated nicely, to secular education, or to economic incentives. It is dangerously to imagine that they will. For this reason, it is the better part of wisdom to exclude foreigners from certain Islamic countries where terrorism is rife, unless one can be assured that those immigrating aspire to America's values and will ultimately successfully assimilate American values.[34]

Sanctuary Cities

The notion of a *sanctuary city* has become fashionable amongst Progressives. Today there are cities, towns, and even states in America that refer to themselves as "sanctuaries" for illegal immigrants. As the concept of a sanctuary city is derived from the Hebrew Bible, so one should consider how the idea was understood in its biblical context. In ancient Israelite society, a sanctuary city—there were five of them—was a lawfully designated location where a man who had *accidentally* caused the death of another—what we might term involuntary manslaughter today—could flee from the vigilante retributive justice of the victim's family. But if the killing was intentional or committed in the context of a crime, the idea of "sanctuary" did not apply. Instead, those individuals were to be promptly captured and delivered to the nearest court, even if they were still clutching at the horns of the "altar" so that they could be duly tried, and if guilty, appropriately punished.

Contrast this with the notion of sanctuary in the Catholic Church. Church canon law suggests that sanctuary applies to *all* who seek it. Indeed, it was judged to be overly punitive to "imprison" fugitives within the confines of a church, and they were allowed to wander freely within a specified distance (Shoemaker, 2011). Here again one encounters the alignment of the *constrained vision* with the teachings of Judaism and the *unconstrained vision* with those of the early Church.

Several Progressive American mayors and governors have openly vowed not to deliver illegal immigrants, including those who have committed serious crimes, to the federal justice system for deportation, an idea

---

34 The difference between traditional Judaism and Christianity is worth noting here. Judaism explicitly allows one to defend oneself, even to the point of killing another who is pursuing you with murderous intent. Christianity emphasizes the need to "love thine enemy." The former values survival; the latter is unconcerned with death.

without precedent in American history, except perhaps during the antebellum period for slaves who escaped to free states. But if there is to be *one law* for citizens and resident aliens, as the Hebrew Bible calls for, then *all* groups must be subject to that law. Illegal aliens have no legal rights under the Constitution, except to be treated humanely. Whereas Progressives argue that deporting them is inhumane, there is no legal or generally agreed upon *moral* basis for that conclusion. There have been several examples in modern times of refugees seeking asylum for urgent reasons of safety who were denied refuge in America. Although those examples may not have been America's "finest hour," laws are meant to be obeyed, and America's *legal* citizens should be of paramount importance. Borders define a nation; they are not provisional, and without them no nation can exist for long. Although what is morally right may be a matter of opinion, in a nation based on laws, beliefs do not trump them.

Laws can be unjust; but in America there are procedures that are meant to be followed if one wishes to change them. In the 1858 Dred Scott decision in the U.S. Supreme Court, slaves were judged not to have rights and were returned to their "legal" masters as chattel. It took the Civil War and an executive order—Lincoln's 1862 Emancipation Proclamation—to abolish slavery. But the problem of antebellum slavery in America is not comparable to the current situation that illegal aliens find themselves in.

The African slave trade was an unfortunate part of early American history, and it has produced serious problems in America for more than 300 years. Despite the blemish that slavery represents for America's history, it was abolished 150 years ago, and progress in civil rights and race relations have rapidly occurred over the last 50 years. A healthy Progressivism would suggest that it is time to move on; but obsessional Progressivism refuses to do so; it is stuck in a psychological net woven from guilt and grudge.

Chapter 8: The Politics of Guilt

All human things are subject to decay, and when
fate summons, monarchs must obey.

—John Dryden, *Mac-Flecknoe*

Psychology of Progressive guilt

Conservative politicians argue that today's Progressivism is a cynical political strategy designed to produce a dedicated voting bloc for the Democratic Party in future elections by creating a welfare system for an underclass of poor and undocumented citizens. Lyndon Johnson, who promoted the legislation of the Great Society in the 1960s, was a practiced politician and personally a known racist. He *did* view the social welfare policies directed at supporting the poor, blacks, and immigrant Hispanics primarily as a strategy for future Democratic Party victories.

But as most ordinary Progressives are not positioned to strategize with respect to future election results, their motives must be sought elsewhere. From a psychodynamic perspective, as Freud noted, the obsessional exhibits a harsh superego directed at failures to achieve childlike notions of perfection. These individuals may have often been held to impossible standards by obsessional parents. They feel guilty about having what they view as unacceptable thoughts and feelings, and for not perfectly meeting the expectations of parents, teachers, and peers. Those who are "successful" continue to live in fear of failing in the future and of losing the approval of others. They feel guilty for the suffering of others, despite having played no role in producing it. Why? Does that stance make any sense? No psychotherapist worth his salt would accept this as a normal reaction.

It can be difficult to distinguish guilt and shame. Guilt generally refers to self-recriminations concerning transgressions against others, whereas shame is a distressing affect that relates to a sudden loss of self-esteem. Narcissists are primarily subject to shame but rarely experience genuine guilt. Today's obsessionals suffer from both. They are hypersensitive about "harming" others while scrupulously avoiding the scrutiny of others or psychological insight. Obsessionals also characteristically exhibit the defense mechanism termed "reaction formation." This was described by Freud and summarized as follows by Calvin Hall (Hall, 1999):

> When one of the instincts produces anxiety by exerting pressure on the ego either directly or by way of the superego, the ego may try to sidetrack the offending impulse by concentrating upon its opposite. For example, if feelings of hate towards another person make one anxious, the ego can facilitate the flow of love to conceal the hostility. (Hall, *Primer*, p. 16)

This means that the outward behavior of the obsessional is often the opposite of their true feelings. Under analytical scrutiny, undue concern about harming others proves to represent a repressed hostile wish to harm others. From a psychoanalytical perspective, the extraordinary lengths that obsessional Progressives go to applaud those who they perceive as disenfranchised belies their contempt toward them as "inferior." The psychoanalyst Wilhelm Reich recognized that one errs in taking the obsessional's "niceties" at face value. What else can one conclude concerning the true feelings of those who promote free speech but then deny it to others on college campuses? Or those who exalt polite behavior but turn a blind eye to the assaults and destruction of property by "Antifa" demonstrators? Conservative pundits explain this as Progressive "hypocrisy," but that may miss deeper psychological motives.

Obsessionals and Authority

As Fromm argued, the obsessional has an uncomfortable ambivalent relationship with authority and rules. Keenly aware of the expectations of others, they often will adhere strictly to rules. But at other times, they can flagrantly disregard them. The conscience of the obsessional is defective. It is experienced as an external "voice" from childhood that whispers imperatives into their ears, concerning what they *should* or *must* do, much like Jiminy Cricket in Walt Disney's *Pinocchio,* who is continually telling the unruly puppet how to behave.

Rules are adhered to because obsessionals think that they might be observed, as they fear being discovered and punished. But when queried in analysis as to how they *really* feel about them, one discovers a distinct lacuna in conscience.

J. was a 36-year-old businessman who was raised in a fundamentalist Seventh Day Adventist family. While he was aware of what was "moral," he admitted to never understanding what the rules were about. When he came to analysis, he was having an affair and afraid of being caught and concerned with what others would think of him. However, he had no desire to end the affair, which was mostly based on pure sexual attraction. He would repeatedly tell me that he knew he was "a bad person" and promise to end his affair, but it was evident that he had no intention of doing so. He was unable to experience genuine guilt and had sociopathic tendencies in other areas as well, including his business dealings.

The psychoanalyst Otto Kernberg suggested that narcissistic individuals exhibit a sector of sociopathy due to their grandiosity, sense of entitlement, and lack of empathy (Kernberg, 1995). The obsessional is rarely an overt sociopath. But covert resistance to rules that were force fed in an authoritarian home or a strict religious environment can result in an unconscious wish to flaunt the rules and, for some, to get caught out doing it. This is especially true if the behaviors of authorities were construed by the child as arbitrary or hypocritical.[35] The patient described above reported that many in his religious community regularly transgressed the strict

---

35 One of the unfortunate features of traditional religions has been the failure to communicate the benefits of religious practice to congregants. In the absence of meaningful communication of these benefits, it can be expected that secularism will replace them.

rules of their religion when "no one was watching."

Why, then, are some obsessional Progressives willing to defy American law? The answer is manifold. First, because of their vulnerability to criticism, obsessional Progressives support policies that allow zero tolerance for criticizing those who they judge as vulnerable in society. This moral imperative aligns well with their neurosis. It allows them to maintain a domain expunged of "aggression" and "unkind" behavior.

Obsessional Progressives perceive themselves as being watched and evaluated by others. They feel pressured in school, by the media, at work, and by peers to behave "correctly." Unduly sensitive to what is expected of them, few critically question whether their values are in fact sound. They participate in a herd mentality and may be too timid to take an independent stand for fear that it might invite criticism. Their choice is either to show support for breaking the law—with the understanding that punitive responses are unlikely in the current political climate—or face criticism and disapproval by their Progressive peers.

Finally, there is the phenomenon of enantiodromia. Obsessionals engaged in doing the "right thing" can undergo sudden and transient psychological shifts that allow them to break the law and engage in what they might otherwise judge as unacceptable behavior.

In Nazi Germany, rules were carefully followed, while what the outside world widely viewed as immoral acts were routinely carried out. The German people feared being shunned by their neighbors and the punitive actions of a murderous regime. But their moral positions were no longer in line with those of the civilized world. As a consequence of being bombarded with propaganda that exacerbated centuries of European anti-Semitism, the German people, not merely the Nazi leaders, were convinced that ridding Germany of its Jews was a *moral* imperative. When notions of morality reverted back at the end of the war, few German citizens accepted responsibility for what had occurred, what philosopher Hannah Arendt termed the "banality of evil."

But despite the diminished importance that Progressives place on laws that oppose their moral ideals, they are inclined to create rules and regulations that control the behavior of others. The Obama Administration imposed more regulations on the financial and private sectors than any previous administration that was not actively engaged in a declared war. This proclivity for regulations applies to Progressive institutions at virtually all levels. Numerous regulations have been created in recent years and vigorously enforced at workplaces, with punitive consequences for those who transgress them. Uniformity of behavior has been fostered by propaganda and digital technologies that allow for the wide-scale monitoring of workers.

Like so many obsessional concerns, the Progressive agenda is laser focused and tends to miss the forest for the trees. Pressing existential issues of national concern are routinely ignored while the rights of minute numbers of minorities have received high priority. America currently faces real political and military challenges from Russia, China, Iran, and North Korea. The Middle East has been left in shambles and a potential training ground for terrorists. The health care system is financially untenable. Many Americans are still unemployed following the recession of 2008, the economy was until recently underperforming, and the country is $20 trillion in debt. These are important existential challenges for America; but Progressives prefer to be preoccupied with who can use a public bathroom.

A cottage industry of institutional bureaucrats has sprouted up, charged with regulating behavior, promoting efficiency, and promulgating the Progressive agenda. Obsessional employees in these institutions are eager to carry out their new charge efficiently, even though compliance invariably reduces their own freedoms. Fromm termed this behavior the "escape from freedom" that is seen in the obsessional "authoritarian personality" (Fromm, 1960).

Those who have been inculcated into the *unconstrained vision* feel guilty concerning the fact that there are vulnerable members in society. But their guilt is ill-founded. As Phillip Rieff suggests with respect to the question of neurotic guilt:

To help us distinguish between guilt on the one hand and a sense of guilt on the other, between responsibility for an offense committed and fantasies about offenses intended or merely imagined, seems a moral as well as a therapeutic aim. To suffer from scrupulosity is after all a well-known perversion of moral ambition, even according to the most elaborate of our established casuistries. (Rieff, *Mind*, p. 174)

This sense of guilt is based on grandiose imaginings of responsibility rather than truth.

For some individuals, the burden of moral perfectionism is difficult to bear. The deleterious role of an overly harsh superego was addressed by Freud in the *Ego and the Id* (S Freud, 1923). He sought to modify the harshness of the superego by determining the unconscious factors that motivate it. Freud never abandoned his support of morality; but he did attempt to distinguish neurotic guilt from real culpability and to alleviate the suffering of those reacting to harsh internalized rules.

Freud's younger colleague, Sandor Ferenczi, a true Progressive in his time, espoused the opinion that any expression of superego in psycho-analysis should be expunged, in both the patient and the analyst (Ferenzci, 1955). According to Ferenczi, neither guilt nor judgment should be part of an analytical treatment. This idea achieved some popularity in the British schools of psychoanalysis, and it is currently widespread in many psycho-therapeutic endeavors and other helping professions.

As noted, Freud adopted much of the metapsychology of psychoanal-ysis from the prohibitions of Judaism (R. Kradin, 2016). The psychana-lytical session is constrained by physical and transactional boundaries. When psychoanalysis became popular amongst British Christian psycho-analysts, elements of the *unconstrained vision* began to emerge both in the theory and practice of psychoanalysis. Concern for how Christian psy-chology might transform psychoanalysis was expressed by the psychoan-alyst Heinz Kohut, the founder of the school of self-psychology, itself a liberal modification of Freud's theory. According to Kohut's biographer (Strozier, 2001):

Kohut felt the goal for revitalizing psychoanalysis was to get the Jews and Protestants to work together. The Jewish medical dominance of psychoanalysis in contemporary America was unfortunate, but if the institutes were dominated by Protestants alone (Kohut thought) it would probably move psychoanalysis toward non-scientific "healing through love" . . . which he saw as unfortunate. (Strozier, *Making*, p.136)

Psychoanalytic treatments informed by the *unconstrained vision* focus on empathy, compassion, forgiveness, and unconditional love, etc., as therapeutic. They systematically ignore the "darker" aspects of human nature, including anger, envy, jealousy, selfishness, which they prefer to see them as aberrations having resulted from having been unsupported, treated punitively, or inadequately loved in childhood. They deny the biological legacy of man's animal nature.

There is little evidence to support the sustained efficacy of purely empathic treatments. Certainly, most individuals will feel temporarily relieved to identify a secure and supportive environment. But there is no evidence that real change results from "unconditional love." If the goal of psychoanalysis is, as the Delphic oracle demanded, to "know thyself," then there is far more to consider than how one may have been aggrieved in childhood. Certainly, ill treatment at any stage of life can evoke pain and leave psychological scars, but it flies in the face of both science and history to conclude that man is pure at heart, and no clear-eyed parent would agree with that conclusion. When the *unconstrained view* permeates society, both truth and society potentially suffer.

This is no less the case for psychotherapists than it is for others. Psychotherapists try to find opportunities to share their clinical experiences with their colleagues. This peer supervision can be extremely helpful, especially around areas where the analyst exhibits persistent "blind spots." The following example suggests how effete a psychological treatment can be when an obsessional psychoanalyst has not been adequately divested of his neurotic defenses:

For several years, I attended a weekly peer supervision conference with my psychoanalytical colleagues. One member of the group was clearly obsessional. He recorded his sessions in painstaking detail with lengthy process notes. Each month, he shared the "progress" that he was making with a middle aged obsessional female patient. Each new session included the patient reporting the same complaints. The analyst's interventions were invariably kind and supportive, but it was evident that no real progress was being made. This continued for several years. Finally, a member of the peer group asked whether the analyst had ever pointed out to the patient that her complaints were neurotically repetitive. His response was, "Oh, I couldn't do that, I don't think that she could tolerate it."

From examples like this, it is easy to understand why insurance companies may refuse to reimburse patients for long-term psychoanalysis. Unfortunately, the art of being an effective psychoanalyst cannot be learned; instead, the empathic capacities and insights required to work productively with patients develop early in life. Obsessional therapists who have not been adequately analyzed with respect to their own resistance to confronting negative affects cannot effect transformative changes in their patients. Instead, they merely collude with the intellectual defenses of their obsessional patients, so that the treatments are both unproductive and interminable.

There is an analysis of the *Grail Legend* by Emma Jung, Carl's wife, herself a psychoanalyst (E. Jung & von Franz, 1998). In one of the versions of the medieval legend, Sir Galahad, having struggled to find the Grail Castle, finally achieves his goal. While in the great room of the Castle, he witnesses a mysterious procession that begs inquiry to be understood. But rather than inquiring about the meaning of what he has observed, Galahad is too polite to ask. Consequently, he awakes the next morning back in the forest and must begin his quest anew. The point is that some issues, especially in psychotherapy, call for inquiry and confrontation. Being overly polite is to be ruled by the aims of society and by one's own hypersensitivities, rather than living authentically.

Shadow

Jung's model of the psyche was based on his experience with images that he encountered in his own dreams and those of his patients in psychoanalysis. He surmised that different aspects of the psyche were symbolized as dream images and that the *shadow* was one observed frequently. In reductive terms, the shadow is comparable to Freud's personal unconscious, but Jung argued that it also included deeper aspects of psychic activity.

Jung argued that the greatest concern for the future of man was reclaiming his *shadow*, for otherwise it must be projected onto others. As he suggests(C. G. Jung, 1970):

> The shadow is a moral problem that challenges the whole ego-personality, for no one can become conscious of the shadow without considerable moral effort. To become conscious of it involves recognizing the dark aspects of the personality as present and real. (Jung, *Aion*, p. 126)

The danger to individual and collective well-being is proportional to how vigorously *shadow* is denied.

President Donald Trump has a host of characterological flaws. He is undoubtedly a narcissist, but few in power at his level are not. But he has been repeatedly labeled a racist, a bigot, a tax evader, an uwitting stooge for Russia's plans to undermine the electoral process, etc. The list goes on, and virtually every day yields some new accusation by those who oppose him. Yet the proof for these accusations has not yet been produced. Psychologically speaking, the fervor and anger with which these accusations are made suggest that they are derived from the split off *shadow* elements of those who have been triggered by Trump's behavior.

Trump frightens obsessional Progressives who fear their own *shadow*. Repeatedly, one hears from Progressives that they are "frightened" by Trump and by his "violent" behaviors. But the reality is that he has done little to merit their fear, other than to provide a "hook" for their projections. Indeed, the Americans who elected him country do not share these concerns and most would eagerly reelect him today as their president based on polls conducted in the states that he carried in the last election. These Americans are not, as Hillary Clinton suggested, "deplorables"; rather, they are Americans weary of political correctness, racial identity politics, excessive regulations, failures to confront the real dangers facing the country, and the pervasive sense of guilt and willingness to concede defeat that characterized the Obama presidency and the Progressive movement. Trump has begun to reverse these policies, as he promised in his campaign, to the glee of some and the unprecedented schadenfreude and resistance of others.

To admit that Barack Obama, America's first black president, was a failure is, for some, both unspeakable and perhaps unthinkable. Yet it is difficult to reconcile the fact that more than 70% of America thought that the nation under Obama's leadership was on the wrong track, whereas his popularity continued to soar to over 60% in polls at the end of his last term. These numbers do not add up any more than the poll numbers did in the recent 2016 presidential election that showed that Trump had no chance of defeating Clinton. The generally proffered reason is that Obama had "charisma," but it is as likely that those who disliked Obama's policies were afraid to admit publicly that they did not approve of his performance, for fear of being labeled as "racists" for criticizing America's first black president. I have treated patients in therapy who report fear of speaking their Conservative views to their Progressive neighbors because they want to avoid vocal disapproval.

But normal individuals recognize that no white person alive today can justly be held responsible for antebellum slavery or the racism of the past in America. Since the sixth century BCE, it has been widely accepted that moral culpability is not inherited. White Americans today were neither slaveholders nor did their immediate forebears participate in the slave trade. It follows that no one living in America today *is*, or should *feel*, guilty for the checkered history of slavery in this country. To feel guilty about events that one has not participated in is a neuroticism, whether one is a white man in

America or a young German in what is no longer Hitler's Third Reich.

Progressives rarely acknowledge that the bulk of the slave trade occurred in black and Islamic sub-Saharan Africa and is still active in some areas of Africa (Horowitz, 2016). White men did not simply capture black slaves on the African continent. Rather they were primarily sold by black African tribal leaders for a profit. It was a dirty business that both whites and blacks participated in. But apparently only white Americans can be held guilty of racial transgressions, a clue to the neurotic guilt and self-loathing that belies this Progressive belief. As Charles Murray notes, the origin of this growing inexplicable guilt is uncertain, but it can be dated to the 1960s and tracks well with the modern Progressive movement (C Murray, 1999).

The idea of a meritocracy, which has been at the core of American moral values, has been dismissed by Progressives as unfair because it does not reward all men equally. It does not matter that some individuals lack intellectual capacities, motivation, or might even be sociopaths, because for Progressives all men *must* be equally deserving and to challenge that "truth" is immoral.

The Talmud describes the events that led to the destruction of the Second Temple by Rome in 70 CE, and ascribes it to the factionalism amongst the Jews. The Rabbis referred to the underlying cause of the destruction as "senseless hatred." The unwillingness of opposing sects to compromise with each other destroyed the Jewish homeland and led to a two-thousand-year diaspora. Americans could stand to learn from this example as to what can potentially happen when civil relationships break down. It is only obsessional rigidity on both sides that prevents cooperation. If left unchecked, it will undoubtedly undermine America's future. But why has America chosen to be on the path toward self-destruction?

Moral Masochism

Psychoanalysts have long recognized that obsessional individuals harbor covert feelings of moral grandiosity. In the *Economic Problem of Masochism* (S Freud, 1924), Freud referred to this dynamic as "moral masochism," and it allowed him to explain why some people appeared to refuse to make improvements in analysis. In such cases, there was a long-standing grudge concerning how they had been treated unfairly as a child by parental figure:

> The satisfaction of this unconscious sense of guilt is perhaps the most powerful bastion in the subject's (usually composite) gain from illness--in the sum of forces which struggle against his recovery and refuse to surrender his state of illness. The suffering entailed by neuroses is precisely the factor that makes them valuable to the masochistic trend. It is instructive, too, to find, contrary to all theory and expectation, that a neurosis which has defied every therapeutic effort may vanish if the subject becomes involved in the misery of an unhappy marriage, or loses all his money, or develops a dangerous organic disease. In such instances one form of suffering has been replaced by another; and we see that all that mattered was that it should be possible to maintain a certain amount of suffering. (Freud, *Economics*, p. 166)

This psychological motif can be identified in the myth of the "dying god" that underlies Christianity. It is exhibited by individuals and groups that feel powerless in the face of perceived mistreatment by powerful authority. The moral masochist will allow himself to be abused and even sacrificed, if he can continue to imagine that he is morally superior to those in power. However, there is an underlying wish in vain hope of being treated fairly and loved. This is often the greatest single impediment to progress in the treatment of obsessional patients in psychotherapy.

Progressives imagine Donald Trump as the embodiment of moral bankruptcy. They deny the legitimacy of the last election, as they are "certain," albeit without evidence, that it could only have been stolen by immoral opponents. They would rather undermine the welfare of the country than admit defeat. The behavior of Progressives is akin to Homer's Achilles, who chose to sit out most of the Trojan War brooding in his tent because he felt he had been unjustly treated. Progressives are self-absorbed in choosing not to engage with the process of governing the country due to their sense of "moral" outrage.

Moral masochism also explains the Obama foreign policy of "leading from behind," and his famous "apology" tour in the Middle East, in which he expressed his apologies for America's having been a powerful but imperfect leader on the world stage. The refusal of Progressives, like Obama, to name and condemn radical Islamic terrorism while denigrating America was not productive. The psychotherapist Howard Schwarz deserves credit for having suggested in his *Revolt of the Primitive* (Schwarz, 2003) that masochism is an element of political correctness that undermines the success of both the government and the private sector.

It is critical to recognize that the stances adopted by Progressives are not simply moral ones; rather, they represent the self-defeating neurotic stance of obsessionals whose ideas of morality have been distorted by perfectionism, envy, hate, and an intractable grudge with America-as-bad-parent. What has transpired in America since the 1960s to foster the self-defeating perceptual distortions of Progressive liberals?

Chapter 9: Politics of Fear

The idea of death haunts the human animal like nothing else, it is a mainspring of human activity.

—Ernst Becker

In his treatise *Denial of Death,* Ernst Becker argues that the psychology of man is imbued with a compulsive need to deny his mortality (Becker, 1973). Linking the notion of the heroic to man's narcissism, he suggests that society is a symbolic system in which "statuses and roles, customs and rules for behavior" are all aimed at achieving imaginal immortality. In earlier times, these symbols were embedded in a matrix of religious ideas and rituals that served to construct meaning out of life. Whether immortality was fostered through the practice of good works or through grace, the survival of the soul was assured.

With the emergence of science and secularism, traditional religious beliefs no longer sufficed to assure that "life" would survive the grave. But when religious beliefs are challenged, so are traditional sources of meaning. Whereas some scholars have argued for centuries that man is innately moral and that a coherent secular morality would have emerged independent of religion, that conclusion remains unproved. According to the philosopher Irving Kristol (Kristol, 1995):

> The philosophical rationalism of secular humanism can at best provide us with a statement of the necessary assumptions of a moral code, but it cannot deliver on any such code itself. Moral codes evolve from the moral experience of communities and can claim authority over behavior only to the degree that individuals are reared to look respectfully even reverently on the moral traditions of their forefathers. It is the function of religion to instill such respect and reverence.

147

(Kristol, *Neoconservatism*, p. 450)

Like other complex psychological expressions, morality has multiple determinants. Morality can reflect a deep-seated reverence for the welfare of others or it can be false and neurotically driven. The main difference between obsessional actions and religious rituals for Freud was that the latter were imbued with meaning for the practitioner, whereas the actions of the neurotic represent frustrated efforts at construing meaning for an existence overwhelmed by anxiety and doubt (S Freud, 1907). However, the distinction may not be as clear if in both cases the underlying aim is to counter existential anxiety, as obsessional rituals also reduce dysphoria; unfortunately, their effects are not long lasting (R. Kradin, 2008).[36]

In *Future of an Illusion*, Freud argued that the religious impulse resists uncontrollable outcomes and the finitude of human life through magical thinking (S Freud, 1927). Many have criticized Freud's simplistic view of religion, which he described as a persistent childhood need to identify with a powerful protective father. This type of thinking was appropriate in a world viewed as dominated by magic. But, Freud argued, religion must now be set aside in favor of reason and science. "The whole thing is so patently infantile, so foreign to reality, that to anyone with a friendly attitude to humanity, it is painful to think that the majority of mortals will never be able to rise above this view of life" (Freud, *Future*, p.138). Freud's appreciation of religion is unsophisticated in many respects; it may reflect the religious beliefs of a simple man but it does not describe those of a theologian. Nevertheless, his recognition of the outward similarities of religious ritual and obsessional neurosis is valid.

Freud's hopes for a new society based on secular humanism and devoid of religious belief have not been achieved. Despite his desire to expunge superstition from the societal *weltanschauung*, religion has merely been replaced by other obsessional systems, including Progressivism.

---

36 In my text *The Placebo Response* (2008, Routledge), I address how obsessional patients may suffer from an inability to self-soothe and achieve states of well-being. Their repetitive behaviors bring transient relief.

This "ism" represents an ideology that views progress as the expression of rationality, science, technology, economic development, and social organization. Those who endorse it, see it—like religion—as the path toward "perfecting" the human condition.

Hegelian notions of progress guided by spirit and the dialogical process of thesis, antithesis, and synthesis, represent an approach in which the old ideas of the past are deconstructed in the order to assure progress (Hegel, 2016).[37](Hegel, 2016) Informed by Christian morality, Progressivism also has a socialist agenda. But in the last eight years under Barack Obama's leadership, it achieved a more intense left-wing *unconstrained vision* than previously seen.

The Progressives of early twentieth century American politics were critical of the Calvinistic "individualism" of the Founding Fathers. Instead of a government that protects individual rights by limited, decentralized power, they envisioned an expansive central government led by intellectual elites and guided by a "living," flexible Constitution. The average individual would not have to participate in political decision making and would instead be free to pursue his potential in other areas, while a concerned government made decisions for him.

In *The Communist Manifesto,* Karl Marx described religion in negative terms (Marx & Engels, 2014). Religion, said Marx, was the "opiate of the people"; its primary role was to aid and abet the exploitation of the working man by a wealthy ruling class. Although Marx's ideas did not take hold in the West, they did form the basis of the atheistic Soviet Union that collapsed in 1989, in some measure in response to the reemergence of religious fervor within the Eastern European bloc.

Despite its Christian roots and purported tolerance of religious freedoms, many Progressives today view institutional religion as an anachronism that impedes progress. For Hegel, it was the nation state not the Church that supported the "divine idea as it exists on earth" (Hegel, 2016).

---

37   The left-wing organization MoveOn.org, financed in large part by the multi-billionaire George Soros, has adopted this motto.

John Burgess, a prominent Progressive political scientist, argued that the purpose of the nation state is the "perfection of humanity, the civilization of the world; the perfect development of the human reason and its attainment to universal command over individualism; the *apotheosis of man*," i.e., man becoming God (Nugent, 2010). The stridency in positions adopted by some liberal Progressives parallel Marxist "religious" intolerance.[38] Short of prohibiting religious practice, Progressivism calls for its reformation in terms that are acceptable to its own ideology.

However, the unconscious religious motifs of Progressives remain essentially undisturbed. Rather than assuming the old forms of divinely directed contemplation and rituals, they manifest as obsessional secular strategies. The reemergence of these motifs is an example of what Freud's referred to as the "return of the repressed."

Freud argued in *Civilization and Its Discontents* that civilized society is a *substitute-formation* (S Freud, 1933). But he then averred that what is repressed as part of the socialization process tends to reemerge, including belief in a transcendent being. Progressivism reflects this repressed motif in its aim of centralizing control over others and participating in "ongoing creation." It is simply the reemergence of religious motifs in secular guise. Obsessional neurosis is characterized by repetitive behaviors that result from repressed ideas and feelings but that continue to influence behaviors due to a lack of insight. Unless self-awareness is achieved, one can expect obsessional strategies to recreate themselves as other ideological "isms."[39]

---

38   In intercepted e-mail conversations of the Clinton campaign manager John Podesta, one of the leaked conversations included the "backwards" ways of the Catholic Church and how something needed to be done to overcome them.

39   Chasidic philosophy speaks of three levels of cognition. The first reflects the initial spar of a new idea (*Chochmah*). This is followed by the ability to discern and develop the idea (*Binah*). Finally, the idea needs to be integrated into the substance of the mind's repertoire (*Daath*). It is this last step that does not occur for the obsessional. As a result, the same ideas reemerge both at the individual and societal levels. There is little real "progress" in Progressivism.

Trauma and Existential Insecurity

Trauma, both physical and psychological, promotes insecurity. What has been termed "stress" in both the lay and psychotherapeutic literature is an ill-defined notion derived from the physical sciences, where it connotes the deformation of a material structure. The term was introduced into common parlance by Hans Selye, a physiologist studying the hormonal reactions of laboratory animals to varying insults in the 1950s (RL Kradin & Benson, 2000). Selye's findings proved to be a great advance in recognizing how the brain and neuroendocrine system react to physical and psychological disturbances.

Studies by Bradford Cannon in the 1930s examined the behavioral reactions of animals to danger, and his findings have informed psychological theorists with respect to the behavioral reactions to stress (Cannon, 1932). Cannon appreciated that when threatened, animals tend to "fight or flight." Subsequent observations demonstrated that some animals also freeze in inaction (e.g., "play possum") or alternatively seek affiliation with others who can provide safety (R. Kradin, 2008). As previously discussed, the primary behavioral strategy of the obsessional is to avoid confrontations a form of mental "flight" or to "freeze" in inactivity (Janet, 1921). But at the societal level, there is also a tendency to "affiliate," safely and at a distance, on social media. Indeed, social media meets all of the psychological demands of the obsessional by allowing him to affiliate while fleeing genuine relationship and to freeze in nonproductive inaction. One can see that such a strategy could prove addictive for the obsessional. The use of social media by Progressive leaders has become the most effective way to spread its propaganda to vulnerable minds. It promotes the opportunity to affiliate with like-minded people who then provide "security" in numbers.

Twenty-first-century America is unquestionably a stressful place, although it may, in fact, be less existentially dangerous than in past times, when societies were regularly ravaged by war and disease. In the post-war 1950s, one could imagine that it was "morning in America," with families sitting in harmony together at the dinner table. But the rapid and constant dissemination of disturbing images over digital media has undermined this tranquility.

Today, those with smart phones—and few do not have them—are constantly barraged by e-mails, alerts, and other signals, all screaming for immediate attention. The reality of a Sabbath or a weekend undisturbed by the demands of the workplace is increasingly rare. America's tranquility has been threatened by Islamic terrorists, an unprecedented wave of violent crime in our inner cities, and an omnipresent background fear of purposeful or error-driven nuclear, biohazard, or power grid apocalypses. The ability to communicate streaming images of war and disaster widely through the media has left individuals with no escape unless they choose to "go off the grid."

Americans are technologically more advanced but less secure than ever. It should come as little surprise that to distract themselves, many spend considerable amounts of time playing video games, watching television, or visiting online pornography sites. Their engagement with virtual realities appears to have made it difficult for Americans to distinguish virtual reality from the real thing. Umberto Eco argued in his monograph *Travels in Hyperreality* that what is without flaws but not real may be more attractive to perfectionists than the coarseness of the material world (Eco, 1990).

Following the cessation of hostilities in World War II, America lapsed into a false sense of invulnerability. It was jolted back to reality by a series of assassinations, including those of President John F. Kennedy, his brother Senator Robert Kennedy, and the civil rights leader Martin Luther King Jr., in the 1960s. This was accompanied a long, unpopular, and unsuccessful war in Vietnam that lasted into the 1970s, punctuated by civil disturbances, and was followed by the precipitous collapse of the Soviet Union in the late1980s. An HIV epidemic left many people fearful for their physical lives and avoidant of sexual intimacy. These events all have contributed to a growing realization amongst complacent Americans that the world is not a predictable, safe place.

But until the Islamic terrorist attack of 9/11/2001, America had been physically isolated from mass destruction on its own soil. On that day, war came home to America. This has been followed by a seemingly interminable threat of terrorism; prolonged wars in Iraq and Afghanistan, which, like Vietnam, have no clear end-game; random mass school shootings; and the gnawing recognition that government is incapable of protecting us. For today's young men who have never had to face conscription into the army, where traditionally "boys became men," and who have been protected from even the minor traumas of daily life, fears can lead to denial, panic, and paranoid ideation.

For the anxious obsessional, the perceived loss of control or the emergence of chaotic affect triggers anxiety that signals the need to reestablish security. Freud recognized that the conscious ego has specific and redundant defenses that protect it from being overwhelmed by anxiety. These were explicated by Anna Freud, based on the works of her father, in *Ego and the Mechanisms of Defense* (A. Freud, 1962).

Persistent stress triggers intellectual rationalizations that can reduce affective discomfort temporarily. But whether they are mediated through fantasies or complex ideologies, they are ultimately fictions based on "magical thinking" (S Freud, 1936). Today, in America, many people live in an illusory bubble that compromises their ability to recognize and respond to real existential threats. In addition to internal psychological defenses, factors external to the individual have been recruited in the service of defending the ego. The Internet today provides endless possible distractions and alternative "realities," through which fearful individuals can escape from unpleasant realities. Walk down the halls of virtually any office in America and you are likely to find workers shopping, playing games online, or "surfing the 'Net."

The ability to deny real existential threat is fostered by postmodern academic scholars who refer to "reality" as a construct that may be interpreted in a variety of ways (Sowell, 2011b). This mode of thinking, as previously discussed, has little practical value; it does not provide "a greater capacity to deal with ambiguity"; rather, it appeals to minds that prefer to retreat into a realm of virtual possibilities.

Adopting Panglossian optimistic narratives in the face of danger is also a mode of neurotic avoidance that can lead to disastrous results. A prime historical example was British Prime Minister Neville Chamberlain's policy of appeasement toward Adolph Hitler's aggression against Czechoslovakia. Chamberlain chose to ignore the clearly expressed aggressive plans of Hitler at Munich to preserve "Peace in our times." It took a world war and a Winston Churchill to snatch Great Britain from the jaws of defeat.

In America, Barack Obama's refusal to identify terrorist threats to the American homeland, his "deals" with the terrorist supporting Iranian regime of mullahs, and his failure to address the serious nuclear challenges raised by a rogue state in North Korea are recent examples of overly optimistic obsessional avoidance and rationalization.

Hypocrisy

It is easy to maintain one's opinion of oneself as a "good" person if one's own flaws are kept at a distance. The psychologist Dan Ariely has made a career out of studying the factors that enhance dishonesty (Ariely, 2012). A genuinely virtuous man who commits a "sin" by lying will soon feel guilty about his transgression. He may initially choose to hide it from others but eventually will confess to clear his troubled conscience. Policemen are aware of this phenomenon amongst those who commit crimes but are not characterological sociopaths.

Contrast that with a Hollywood starlet who may advocate for the rights of poor black workers in Mississippi, or for combatting global warming. Likely having never having met or spent time with a black worker in Mississippi, and apparently unconcerned about increasing her carbon footprint while jetting around the world, her words do not translate into actions. Her physical and psychological *distance* from both situations allows her to believe that her moral standards are sincere. Is she a hypocrite? Perhaps, but to put it more generously—and possibly accurately—she is accomplished at maintaining the illusion that she is not deceiving herself, precisely because she is sufficiently removed from the realities she professes concern for.

Furthermore, one should not forget that many in Hollywood are actors, and the psychology of those who choose to act for a living is an area of complexity that cannot be addressed here. Suffice it to say, their expertise in the political realm is usually limited, and they are generally no more qualified to express opinions on such matters than less celebrated citizens.

Chapter 10: The Language of Deception

In the beginning was the Word, and the Word
was with God, and the Word was God.

—Prologue to the Gospel of John

The potential for obsessionality emerged with human consciousness and man's wish to control his world. Ancient creation myths emphasize how order was imposed upon unruly chthonic forces. In the absence of self-reflective thought and speech, man differs little from other animals.[40] The evolution of society, and more broadly civilization, hinges on language. Words, originally signifiers of objects in the material world, are now used regularly to represent ideas that may be far removed from tangible reality.

Language can be used tin the service of constructing symbolic systems. These *ideologies* can fascinate but they may also mislead. As Hannah Arendt explains in *Origins of Totalitarianism* (Arendt, 1976):

> An ideology is quite literally what its name indicates: it is the logic of an idea. Its subject matter is history, to which an "idea" is applied; the result of this application is not a body of statements about something that is, but the unfolding of a process which is in constant change. . . . Ideologies pretend to know the mysteries of the whole historical process—the secrets of the past, the intricacies of the present, the uncertainties of the future—because of the logic inherent in their respective ideas. (Arendt, *Origins*, p. 176)

---

40 Judaism refers to four categories of earthy existence: inorganic matter (*domeh*), plant life (*tzomeh*), animal life (*chai*), and man who "speaks" (*medaber*), emphasizing the unique quality of human thought and speech.

As Arendt explains, ideologies can be rational but they are invariably limited in their ability to explain the real world with accuracy. They are simplistic, as they derive from a single or limited number of core concepts, which are then awkwardly imposed on complex realities. Arendt continues:

> The claim to total explanation promises to explain all historical happenings, the total explanation of the past, the total knowledge of the present, and the reliable prediction of the future. Secondly, in this capacity ideological thinking becomes independent of all experience from which it cannot learn anything new even if it is a question of something that has just come to pass. (Arendt, *Origins*, p. 203)

In this respect, ideologies are potential resistances against accepting experiencing reality, as such. They are explanatory structures that serve to contain societal angst, much in the same way that thought may limit an individual's anxiety. Unfortunately, the conclusions drawn from them are generally false when too broadly applied. Yet once entrenched, like mathematical attractors, ideologies resist alternative explanations.

The neurotic obsessional thinks *too* much. His mind is driven by excessive cognitions (Association, 1994; Ingram & May 1961). He responds to anxiety with a limited number of narratives that fail to consider the complexities of real experience. Although his anxiety may be contained by ideology, his ability to learn and respond adaptively to new experience or information is impaired.

In the past, ideologies were created by intellectuals and then slowly disseminated either by word of mouth or in books to a limited number of followers. Today, however, ideologies can be widely disseminated as propaganda via the mainstream news and social media, so that large segments of society have rapidly come to share simplistic beliefs that resist alternative explanations. The widespread dissemination of ideology fosters a herd mentality and "groupthink." Many Americans today find it impossible to question the ideology of Progressivism without fear of being criticized or punished by friends, colleagues, and institutions. As Arendt suggests:

The propaganda of the totalitarian movement also serves to eman-cipate thought from experience and reality; it always strives to inject a secret meaning into every public, tangible event and to suspect a se-cret intent behind every public political act. (Arendt, *Origins*, p. 304)

It may be difficult to discern the creeping totalitarian agenda of Pro-gressivism, as many are too close to it to see clearly and cannot believe that it could happen in America. But the current face of Progressivism me-diated by political correctness has grown uncomfortably close to Arendt's description of totalitarianism. This should concern Americans, regardless of their political affiliations.

Scholarship

Prior to the Internet, a scholar was generally a well-read storehouse of information. But access to the Internet has changed this. Young scholars often rely primarily on websites like Wikipedia as their primary source of information. It offers immediate access to a universe of superficial in-formation but rarely provides the perspective that one gains from reading authored texts.

Young scholars counter that it is inefficient to store information in one's own memory when it can be readily accessed elsewhere. But the result of this approach limits in-depth understanding of a field. This argu-ment is relevant with respect to determining who is qualified to comment on what is transpiring in society. Few scholars today are polymaths. As Sowell notes, a professor of sociology likely has little basis to comment intelligently on economics. One must wonder to what extent intellectuals espousing opinions on virtually all topics merit serious attention. And if this is true of scholars, how much more so is it for those in the entertain-ment or sports industries? Unfortunately, American politics has increas-ingly become a popularity contest, with film and TV celebrities running for the highest offices, and in some cases winning them.

Knowledge as Power

The idea that "knowledge is power" holds strong appeal for the obsessional. In the history of religion, Gnosticism, a second-century CE Middle Platonic Christian philosophy, espoused the view that salvation could only be achieved via the acquisition of esoteric knowledge. Gnostics divided mankind into the *pneumatikoi*, an elite that would ultimately be saved via their knowledge, the *psychikoi,* those with less intellect but who might still merit salvation with effort, and those who could never achieve salvation, the fleshy *sarkikoi.* What eventually became Christian orthodoxy rejected Gnosticism as elitist, as it undermined the hope of salvation for those who had faith in the resurrection of Christ. As Paul warned in Colossians 2:8:

> See to it that no one takes you captive through philosophy and empty deceit, according to human tradition, according to the elemental spirits of the universe and not according to Christ.

Platonic philosophies like Gnosticism share with the obsessional neurotic a striving for power, perfection, and an abhorrence of the physical. The quest for salvation through knowledge has reemerged in the modern myth of Progressivism, in which an intellectual elite imagines itself as best suited to rule. This includes most scholars in academia, journalists, and information technologists, the Google, Apple, Facebook, etc. community. Currently, this "elite" has joined forces in a virulent no-holds-barred campaign against the new president and those who espouse Conservative views in general. From their perspective, unenlightened "fleshy" Conservatives should have little to say about America's future. But much of America disagrees.

Chapter 11: Progressivism: A Very Short History

A great democracy has got to be progressive or it will soon cease to be great or a democracy.

—Theodore Roosevelt

These times are too progressive. Everything has changed too fast. Railroads and telegraphs and kerosene and coal stoves—they're good to have but the trouble is, folks get to depend on 'em.

—Laura Ingalls Wilder

As the term suggests, Progressivism developed as an ideology based on the notion of progress. The ideology of Progressivism can be traced to the eighteenth-century German philosopher Georg Wilhelm Friedrich Hegel, who argued that history is moved by divine Spirit, enacted through the workings of the state for the purpose of perfecting society. Other twentieth-century ideologies, including Socialism, Fascism, and Communism also espoused notions of progress and societal improvement, but it was Progressivism that took hold in America (Nugent, 2010).

Progressivism has been the reigning political philosophy in America for more than a century. It emerged after Federalism proved unable to preserve the Union when States' rights opposed the will of the federal government, leading to the Civil War. After the war, the federal government found its powers greatly enhanced. The idea emerged that a strong but well-intentioned central government, one led by an intellectual and charismatic elite, would be best positioned to determine the public good.

Woodrow Wilson

Since at least 1913, the liberal interpretation of the American system of government has been under assault by Progressives from both major American parties. Both Theodore Roosevelt, a Republican, and Woodrow Wilson, a Democrat, championed Progressive ideas during the presidential campaign of 1912 (Berg, 2013). With Wilson's election, the powers and role of the federal government increased.

Wilson was the first academic to be elected president of the United States, and he held a doctorate in the new field of political science. He espoused strong views concerning the role and direction of government, arguing that government's aim was the progressive perfection of society, in response to its rapidly changing needs. For Wilson and other Progressives, the direction of government would be determined in concert by an elite group of politicians and a charismatic president, who served as the instrument of effecting progress by the federal government. All aspects of society are required to participate in the Progressive vision, including the nation's educational systems. The Constitution, which from a traditional liberal perspective was designed to ensure the rights of the individual, would no longer be considered a static document but a "living" one, to be reinterpreted and even ignored when it was perceived to no longer meet the needs of society.

Wilson oversaw the passage of progressive legislative policies, including the Federal Reserve Act, Federal Trade Commission Act, the Clayton Antitrust Act, and the Federal Farm Loan Act. He initiated the Revenue Act of 1913, which introduced a graded income tax and lower tariffs. He imposed an eight-hour workday for the railroad workers. Although he campaigned in 1916 for a second term on the platform of remaining neutral in the Great War in Europe, he soon reversed his promise and brought America into the War. At its end, Wilson promoted his 14-point policy that became the basis for the League of Nations, the forerunner of the current United Nations.

Wilson's Progressive policies sought to consolidate power to promote the Progressive agenda. The Wilson administration also proposed a constitutional amendment to prohibit the purchase and consumption of alcoholic beverages, commonly referred to as "Prohibition." Although he supported women's voting rights, he did so with some reticence. But Wilson was also an Old South segregationist who voiced his antipathy toward the notion of equal rights for African Americans.

The New Deal

The next major phase in American Progressivism occurred during the four terms of President Franklin D. Roosevelt (Dallek, 2017). Roosevelt idolized his vigorous Progressive cousin Theodore and had been Wilson's Secretary of the Navy. He was elected to the White House while America was immersed in the Great Depression. His response to the crisis was to centralize power in Washington via a series of legislative programs collectively called the New Deal. Historians refer to the "First New Deal" (1933–34) and a "Second New Deal" (1935–38). The "First New Deal" dealt primarily with the banking crises.

The "Second New Deal" promoted labor unions, the Works Progress Administration (WPA), a relief program that made the federal government the largest single employer in the nation, and the Social Security Act, an intergenerational Ponzi scheme designed to ensure the income of retirees, and new programs to aid tenant farmers and migrant workers.

The New Deal included both new legislation and a proliferation of executive orders that were issued unilaterally by Roosevelt. Conservative critics questioned his policies and the consolidation of power within the presidency. By the middle of his second term, criticism of Roosevelt centered on fears that he was steering America toward a dictatorship. In order to overcome legal challenges to the constitutionality of his social reform programs, he attempted to pack the Supreme Court in 1937 with sympathetic jurists, but his attempts were blocked.

The scope of the Progressive reforms instituted by Roosevelt introduced elements of socialism previously unseen in America, and many of the policies of the progressive New Deal remain in place today. These include the Federal Deposit Insurance Corporation (FDIC), the Federal Crop Insurance Corporation (FCIC), the Federal Housing Administration (FHA), and the Tennessee Valley Authority (TVA), as well as the Social Security System and the Securities and Exchange Commission (SEC). This transformation of American domestic policy has resulted in implicit acceptance of Progressive policies in America, even amongst many Conservatives.

The centralization of power in Washington, D.C., included executive orders that violated the freedoms of American citizens. In 1942, Roosevelt issued Executive Order 9066, which applied to everyone classified as an "enemy alien," including people with dual citizenship living in designated high-risk areas. Some 120,000 people of Japanese ancestry were held in internment camps from 1942 to 1945.

Lyndon Johnson's Great Society

Lyndon Johnson assumed the presidency following the assassination John F. Kennedy in 1963. A seasoned politician and former Senate Majority leader, Johnson had served in the Roosevelt administration (Goodwin, 1991). His ability to move legislation through Congress resulted in the greatest advances in the Progressive agenda since Roosevelt. Johnson's first public reference to the "Great Society" took place in a speech in 1964: "...we will build a Great Society. It is a Society where no child will go unfed, and no youngster will go unschooled."

Johnson was a shrewd politician who understood how to wield and consolidate power. Much of his legislation was aimed at ensuring the civil rights of minorities with the additional benefit of courting a new voting bloc for the Democratic Party. Johnson's efforts greatly enhanced the rights of African Americans in this country. The Civil Rights Act of 1964 forbade job discrimination and the segregation of public accommodations. The Voting Rights Act of 1965 ensured minority registration and voting. The Immigration and Nationality Services Act of 1965 abolished quotas in immigration law and has led to problems that are currently at the center of America's political conflicts.

The War on Poverty created an Office of Economic Opportunity to oversee a variety of community-based antipoverty programs. Federal funds were targeted toward providing special education schemes in slum areas, and financial aid was also provided for inner city renovations. The Food Stamp Act of 1964 expanded the federal food stamp program. The Elementary and Secondary Education Act of 1965 provided significant federal aid to public education and programs targeting low-income children.

The Social Security Act of 1965 authorized Medicare and federal funding to defray the medical costs of older Americans. The legislation overcame the bitter resistance to the idea of publicly funded health care or "socialized medicine." Welfare recipients of all ages received medical care through the Medicaid program. These massive legislative efforts fostered Progressive ideology. They consolidated power in the hands of the federal government, introduced a new and unprecedented level of control on matters previously determined by the states and the private sector, and introduced large numbers of new voters who were beholden to the Democratic Party for providing tangible benefits in all sectors of private life. The Progressive goal of a socialized welfare state was no longer a dream.

Bill Clinton and the Culture Wars

William Jefferson Clinton succeeded President George H. W. Bush in 1992. Clinton was dedicated to the Progressive agenda but in general adopted a centrist approach to his presidency (Klein 2002). Shortly after taking office, he reversed restrictions on domestic family planning programs. He cut taxes for low-income families while raising taxes on the wealthiest taxpayers. With his wife, Hillary Clinton, he proposed a national health care plan that failed to gain legislative support. He signed the Brady Bill, which mandated federal background checks on firearm purchases and imposed a five-day waiting period. Clinton implemented a directive known as "Don't Ask, Don't Tell," which allowed gay men and women to serve in the armed services, provided they kept their sexual preferences a secret, concomitantly forbidding the military from inquiring about individual sexual orientation.

Clinton was responsible for pressing federal agencies, the courts system, and the military onto the Internet. In 1996, he issued an executive order ordering all federal agencies to utilize information technology to make information accessible to the public. Clinton issued executive orders on behalf of gay rights, the first lifting the ban on security clearances for lesbian, gay, bisexual, and transsexual (LGBT) federal employees and the second outlawing discrimination based on sexual orientation in the federal workforce.

During his presidency, the stalemate between the conservative Congress and the liberal executive branch reached a new fervor. Conservatives favoring strict constitutional interpretation, traditional values, and free trade pitted themselves in opposition to the Progressive values of the Clinton administration, going so far as to impeach him in the House of Representatives for personal misconduct, although he was subsequently acquitted in the Senate.

George W. Bush

The presidency of George W. Bush was in large measure defined by the War on Terror. However, opposition to Bush's policies, both domestic and international, was widely argued by liberal Progressives (Smith, 2016). However, Bush referred to himself as a "compassionate Conservative" and on some important matters his policies continued the Progressive agenda.

Bush was challenged as an off-the-cuff politician. His answers to journalists' questions were simple and often awkwardly phrased. He was clearly not a member of the glib intellectual elite. With time, Progressives became increasingly vocal in their opposition to Bush's policies, openly demonizing the president and his policies. Bush would leave office demoralized by consistent attacks on his intelligence, character, and policies.

Barack Obama and the Progressive Left

Barack Obama assumed the reins of government from President George W. Bush, inheriting the ongoing "War on Terror" and a financial crisis of major proportions. He continued the bailout of failing America financial institutions imposed by his predecessor to stabilize the economy.

Obama was distinguished by being the first African American to gain the presidency, although he had accomplished little in his short career in the Senate (Garrow, 2017). His experience had been primarily gained as a leftist community organizer. His mentors were Progressives, some with radical leftist views. Obama and his Secretary of State, Hillary Clinton, were both ideological followers of Saul Alinsky, a socialist activist who argued that to transform capitalist American society into a socialist state, tactics should be formulated that can appeal to the masses. Dishonesty with the American people in the service of what was perceived as moral imperatives was justified according to Alinsky, but foul language and protesting on the streets would not be as effective as lasting legislative changes (Alinsky, 1971). Obama studied the works of Alinsky and embraced his approach.

The result was a sharp turn to the left in American politics with emphases on gender issues and identity politics. Obama proved to be the most left-leaning Progressive president in American history, promoting an agenda that challenged both the constitutional system and the idea of American exceptionalism on the world stage. Articulate and charismatic, Obama enjoyed the widespread support of the left-leaning mainstream press, academics, and peoples of color, all of whom appeared hard pressed to recognize, or accept criticism of the president's policy misadventures. Despite virtually no record of accomplishment in foreign affairs, he was awarded the Nobel Peace Prize in the first year of his presidency.

After eight years in office, Obama left America deeply polarized around issues of race, culture, and religious beliefs, with the lowest GDP growth since the Great Depression, and high unemployment with respect to full time well-paying jobs. His international and domestic security positions have been strongly criticized by Conservatives, and it is virtually certain that most of his policies will be reversed by the new Trump presidency, as they were enacted by executive orders rather than through legislative consensus.

Obama's greatest legislative achievement was the Affordable Care Act (Obamacare), which mandated health care for all Americans through a complex synthesis of private and public insurance. Conservative detractors viewed it as an imposition on the public and as economically nonviable. Despite certain elements that were publicly popular, such as mandated health care for the poor and those with preexisting health conditions, the bill was structured in a fashion that would likely lead to its collapse, hopefully, for some liberal Progressives, to be replaced by a single-party payer socialized medicine comparable to that in most liberal socialist countries in the West.

The Obama administration increased regulations on businesses while maintaining high tax rates for individuals and small businesses. The rate of economic growth over his eight-year presidency reached historical lows. The rate of unemployment for blacks and Hispanics was unprecedentedly high. In addition, Obama managed to add more to the national debt—currently $20 trillion and rising—than *all* previous presidential administrations combined.

Obama's stance on foreign policy was a sharp departure from that of previous American administrations. He exhibited little appetite for exercising power on the international scene, and left a vacuum for Islamic terrorism to spread through a fractured Middle East. He was notably unwilling to ascribe the wave of terrorism in America and the West to fundamentalist Islam, despite overwhelming evidence for the attribution. He lifted economic sanctions on Iran and signed a hugely expensive treaty to limit nuclear development with its fundamentalist anti-American leaders, all without the approval of Congress. He failed like his predecessors to intervene to block the development of nuclear weapons in North Korea that may be able to reach the mainland of the United States in the near future.

Obama failed to react to the scourge of black on black crime in the inner cities, preferring instead to focus on identity politics, thereby adding to distorted perceptions of white "racism" that have become prevalent amongst liberal Progressives. Finally, although he did actively deport illegal aliens entering through the southern border, he refused to aggressively prosecute crimes committed by illegal aliens within the country.

Whereas Obama's rhetoric soared with inspiration and hope, he was widely perceived as "cold," overly rational, and slow to respond when required. His presidency appeared to flounder from crisis to crisis. A rigid ideologue, he showed little capacity to compromise with his political opponents. He broke with American tradition and law by unilaterally enacting virtually his entire agenda through executive orders, recognizing that some orders, like the Deferred Action for Children of Illegal Aliens Act (DACA), the so-called "Dreamer Act," were unconstitutional.

Obama's inability to accept personal criticism was evident in his unwillingness to accept responsibility for any of the serious failings of his Administration, although he did at the end of his term reticently admit to being disappointed with the outcome of his policies in the Middle East. He blamed the Republican legislative branch for blocking his proposed legislation and appointments, although he had made little effort at cooperating with them. Inordinately concerned with his "legacy" in history, Obama created a rationalized narrative that refused to acknowledge that his policies had been rejected by most of the American electorate outside the urban bastions of Progressivism.

The eight years of Obama's presidency witnessed a sharp divide in the culture wars and identity politics of America. His personal contributions to the current conflict were substantial, but he was by no means the sole agent of change. The other factors responsible for these changes must be considered before a balanced summary can be achieved.

Chapter 12: Feminism and Identity Politics

God may be in the detail, but the Goddess is in connection.

—Gloria Steinem.

Where love reigns, there is no will to power; and where the will to power is paramount, love is lacking. The one is but the shadow of the other.

—C.G. Jung

What Do Women Want?

The rise of the feminist movement has had a profound effect on America and on the focus of Progressivism. It has profoundly influenced ideas concerning what is acceptable in society, as well as how obsessionality manifests in society.

Freud—always unpopular with feminists—famously stated in a letter to his protégée Marie Bonaparte: "The great question that has never been answered, and which I have not yet been able to answer, despite my thirty years of research into the feminine soul, is 'What does a woman want?'"

The aims of feminism have been a moving target. In her introduction to *Modern Feminist Theory*, Jennifer Rich refers to a conversation that she overheard at a women's discussion group, in which members of the group were attempting to define the major goals of feminism (Rich, 2007):

Some... suggested that feminism was the demand for "equal rights"; some that it involved the dismantling of the "sex/gender" system; still others that it was an unending struggle against male domination in all of its forms. Finally, an eight-year old girl who had been listening intently to the conversation asked the following—"Isn't feminism the belief that women are human beings?" (Rich, *Introduction to Feminism*, p. 1)

The young girl's suggestion ideally might be the correct answer, but some feminists continue to profess hostility toward men, arguing that equality has not yet been achieved. But men and women are not "equal."

Gender differences have been demonstrated in virtually all credible scientific studies on the topic, although to speak of them is risky, as the former president of Harvard Lawrence Summers discovered when he correctly noted that women in general do not excel at the hard sciences. Summers was forced to resign for daring to speak that truth. Summers would later comment: "There is a great deal of absurd political correctness. Now, I'm somebody who believes very strongly in diversity, who resists racism in all of its many incarnations, who thinks that there is a great deal that's unjust in American society that needs to be combated, but it seems to be that there is a kind of creeping totalitarianism in terms of what kind of ideas are acceptable and are debatable on college campuses" (Summers, 2016).

In a 2011 research study by Weisberg and co-workers (Weisberg, DeYoung, & Hirsh, 2011), women scored higher on personality scales for extraversion, agreeableness, and neuroticism than men, with significant gender differences appearing in aspects of every major personality trait.

Popular books like John Gray's *Men are from Mars, Women are from Venus* have addressed the different cognitive relational style differences of the sexes (Gray, 2012). In Freud's time, prior to the emergence of feminism, obsessionality was generally viewed as a masculine personality style, whereas the hysterical style was attributed to women. Indeed, it was vehemently argued in that male hysteria never occurred.[41] Yet women have always exhibited obsessional styles—consider the Germanic *haus-*

---

41 Freud was jeered by his Viennese colleagues when he attempted to present a paper on a case of male hysteria, so anathema was the idea at the time.

frau obsessed with cleaning and order. On close analytical observation, obsessionality frequently co-exists with hysterical motifs in both men and women. Some highly emotional women appear to exhibit the hysterical style, but they may also exhibit areas of obsessionality in sectors of their life.

Indeed, the obsessional woman is commonplace today. Obsessional women present to analysis often with blunted affect and intellectual defenses. They may remark that they find the analytical process "interesting" rather than emotionally transformative. In my personal analytical experience, they may describe having been close with their fathers, and treated more like a "son than a daughter." Some seek out well-published male analysts from whom they can "learn," with the underlying desire of recreating the early father-daughter intellectual intimacy and identifying a "mentor." Many have described negative relationships with their mothers and other women, and they may express contempt for women who are "vague," "mixed-up," or "incompetent."

Like obsessional men, obsessional women are often invested in their work. Some choose not to marry or have children, whereas others attempt to fit children into an impossibly busy work schedule, juggling nannies and other obligations between work and home.

Women and Relationships

Jung referred to *Eros* as the capacity for relationship and suggested that as a rule women are more adept at it than men, and this observation has been confirmed in most modern studies of gender (C. G. Jung & Jaffe, 1959). Women's capacity for attachment and relationship is likely biologically hard-wired. Neurobiological observations suggest that maternal hypothalamic release of the hormone oxytocin plays a critical role in initiating attachment to the newborn suckling infant (Sapolsky, 2017).

Women may exhibit difficulties in setting firm boundaries in relationships. They may be more opposed to the imposition of strict boundaries than men, be they the enforcement of laws or the setting of secure national boundaries.

The feminist author Carol Gilligan argues in *In a Different Voice* that women tend to make decisions with greater consideration of how they affect the feelings of others (Gilligan, 1999). She criticized Kohlberg's argument that girls on average reach a lower level of moral development than boys. She countered that Kohlberg tended to favor a principled way of reasoning, one more common to boys, over moral arguments based on relationships that are more amenable to girls.

According to Gilligan, there are two types of moral voice. The masculine voice is "logical and individualistic." Its primary concerns are protecting the individual rights of people and ensuring that justice is done. By contrast, the female voice emphasizes the importance of compassionate care and the protection of others. The overlap between the feminine "moral voice" and the *unconstrained vision* of today's Progressivism is not coincidental. Nor is it a great leap to the strategies of political correctness, which also originated in feminist thought.

Feminism has profoundly influenced the current direction of Progressive ideology. It has helped to move it to the left of what had traditionally been termed "liberalism." The Progressive agenda currently runs strongly counter to Conservative ideology. Whereas America's political conflict certainly cannot be framed simply as a "battle of the sexes," it does parallel the polar agendas of feminism and what one might call for want of a better term "masculinism." Whereas few men today would openly object to the equitable treatment of women or minorities, some still balk at the feminist movement's support of LGBT rights, open borders, sanctuary cities, identity politics, etc. However, that is also changing as more men feel compelled to speak with a feminine voice.

Women and Empathy

Psychoanalysis has in recent years been less interested in Freud's one-body theory of mind that emphasized the intersubjective dynamic between consciousness and the unconscious, and has instead focused on the importance of interpersonal relational dynamics. Infant psychological research has demonstrated the apparent importance of empathic attunement and attachment between mothers and infants (Stern, 1985). Object relations, *self-psychology,* and attachment theory all emphasize the role of early mothering as a factor in determining an adult's capacity to be empathic to others versus narcissistically self-absorbed.

But what is genuine empathy? The answer merits consideration. The self-psychologist Heinz Kohut (1971) referred to empathy as "vicarious introspection" (i.e., the psychologically capacity to intuit the experience of others accurately). This is not a simple task; it requires the ability to discern what another is experiencing while at the same time distinguishing one's own feelings from those of another.

There is little evidence that empathy is developed at birth. Although some may be born with a greater capacity for empathy, like most inherited psychological capacities, it must be nurtured early in life; it cannot be taught or learned as an adult. It likely requires a well-attuned mother if one is to recognize empathically the overtly expressed and implicit cues communicated by others.

I have had the experience (as someone who trains psychoanalysts) to encounter some who have no apparent talent for reading the minds of others, although they may be strongly attracted to helping them. I have occasionally suggested tactfully that some might be better served in another profession. My Progressive colleagues have criticized me for this stance, as they believe, without evidence, that virtually anything can be taught. The result in some cases has been more than a few individuals who have remained in training for more than ten years. Some eventually graduate; others leave in frustration, having wasted a great deal of time and money. Many of the trainees with these problems have significant obsessional or narcissistic issues.

The empathy of obsessionals is impaired, as it is in all rigid personality types. Obsessional mothers tend to project their own inner states inappropriately onto their children, which results in repeated empathic failures. This can be seen, for example, in some women who exhibit an obsession with food. Their first reaction as mothers to infant distress is to assume that the child is hungry, but they may fail to consider other possible causes of discomfort when feeding does not comfort the child.

Rather than being empathic, obsessionals instead are predisposed to exhibiting "sympathy" for others. Sympathy is often based on projections of repressed memories of loss and abandonment affects. It is an *asymmetric* response that imagines others as unduly vulnerable, which is the self-experience that obsessionals work hard at disavowing. By projecting it onto others, the obsessional maintains illusions of invulnerability. A psychoanalytic supervisor once counseled me that obsessional patients can resist therapeutic insight for years, but their fear of abandonment is sufficiently profound that once they make an attachment in therapy, they rarely leave it.

Whereas feelings of sympathy are part of the unconscious repertoire of both obsessional women and men, they may be heightened by women's natural proclivity for relationship. But when repressed feelings of abandonment and rejection are not consciously recognized, they can distort relationships and surface in ways that are experienced by others as condescension.

A young obsessional female physician was friendly with several "gay" men and chose to vacation overseas with one of them. She prided herself on being "unprejudiced" and supportive of her friend's gay lifestyle. The behavior of gay men reportedly "amused" her. But after returning from the trip, her gay male friend refused to have anything more to do with her. He claimed that her behavior on the trip had been consistently condescending. She had no idea what he was referring to.

How, then, does empathy differ from sympathy? The distinction has not been formally established, but I suggest the following operative distinction. Genuine *empathy* includes not only the ability to intuit accurately the mental experience of another, as Kohut suggested, but also includes genuine *concern* for their welfare. The object of empathy should experientially benefit from being understood. Genuine empathy is therefore therapeutic, whereas sympathy is not. Rather, the latter is either enabling or condescending. This is often the distinction made between a mother and an unrelated caretaker (R. L. Kradin, 1997).

When a young child falls and hurts his knee, it is callous not to empathically acknowledge his pain. But as accidents do happen, it is also in the child's interests to learn to absorb some degree of discomfort in stride. Genuine empathy conveys both messages. It is one thing to express concern for one who is suffering, quite another to encourage that person to adapt to the vicissitudes of life. The former response is sympathy, the latter, genuine empathy. Sympathy in fact often represents misattunement, projection, and judgment. It is never therapeutic because only the sympathizer truly benefits. I am not suggesting that there is no role for sympathy. We all have been in situations where sympathetic condolences are called for. But when properly offered, they are closer to what has been described here as empathy.

Empathic concern is a feature of a highly refined morality. It considers both the individual and the welfare of the community. But in a country based on law, as America has traditionally been, the rule of law must be dispassionate. It must favor neither the rich nor the poor. The well-being of the society must be considered. Proper punishment for bad behavior in many cases *is* empathic, as it considers the possibility that the individual may *wish* to be helped to behave better, and it also protects those who are innocent and have been wronged. There is a role in society for tough love if it includes genuine concern.

Newspapers regularly report on serious crimes committed in America that go unpunished or lightly so. Progressives appear to be inclined to coddle lawbreaking aliens and minorities because they perceive them as disadvantaged or in need of therapy not punishment. But this stance is neither "just" nor empathic; it is, from the perspective presented here, also immoral.

In a recent case in liberal Boston, a young African man on a temporary visa was convicted of engaging in two bank robberies in which he threatened to kill people in the bank if he did not get the money he was seeking. He was apprehended, allowed to plea bargain, and served a brief sentence for a serious crime so that he would not have to face deportation. Shortly after being released back into society, he brutally murdered two young Boston physicians.

Unfortunately, crimes like this occur with some frequency in Progressive America because it is judged as too harsh to punish individuals appropriately. But the victims—two young, productive physicians—were not considered in this calculus because of the wish to forgive criminal aliens out of some misguided sense of neurotic guilt. Obsessional ideology allows Progressives to discount the importance of individuals for what they perceive as a "higher moral good."

I live in a town in Massachusetts that is home to at most a handful of minorities; it is an affluent white suburb where many Harvard academics and wealthy businessmen reside. One can see innumerable "Black Lives Matter" signs on churches, houses, and lawns in the town. Whereas there is nothing intrinsically wrong with this, their position might be more convincing if there were, in fact, *real* diversity in the town.

Nor does the Progressive argument that most illegal aliens are law abiding merit serious consideration. The legal system cannot be called upon to discern the difference between those who "seriously" break the law and those who are otherwise "law abiding" but nevertheless are here illegally. And if the feminine psyche, as Gilligan suggests, is unable to make "principled" rather than "relational" decisions, then perhaps it might be best for "relational" types, be they men or women, or like-minded men might best avoid working in the legal profession unless they are willing to bear the responsibility for the fate of those who are victimized as the consequence of overly lenient prosecutions and sentencings. In addition, the Progressive press that repeatedly chooses to hide certain crimes from public view, when uncomfortable truths of the case challenge their ideology, must also bear responsibility for the harm done to others in neglecting to report the facts. The role of the press is to inform the public about the facts so that they can remain apprised of it and make its own conclusions concerning how justice is meted out today.

The various sectarian divisions within the major religions in America today are also divided concerning the *constrained* and *unconstrained* visions. Whereas all the monotheistic religions include an emphasis on social justice, liberal Progressivism colors the priorities of the more liberal sects and denominations. Rabbi Joseph Soloveichik, one of the major thinkers in Orthodox Judaism in the twentieth century, weighed in on this issue by examining the differences between secular and religious morality.

Traditional Judaism makes distinction between different types of laws. Some laws have apparent explanations; others, such as the purity laws, do not, yet both must be obeyed as a matter of faith.[42] But how to interpret the law is not simple. As Soloveichik (2005) argues:

> There is a law against theft. . . . Everyone assents to such a law . . . . every normal person is repelled by the ugliness of the act. . . . No one will approve of stealing candy from a baby or money from a beggar. But what about another sort of theft, which was depicted so often in literature, particularly by Victor Hugo in *Les Miserables*? A poor man, just out of prison, with no prospects, steals a loaf of bread from a bakery in order to sustain his life. The proprietor of the bakery . . . will not suffer. The loss occurred is infinitesimal. Why punish the poor

---

42   As I am writing this, a new announcement was issued by the U.S. Attorney General that federal law that bans marijuana will be enforced in states that have now chosen to legalize "pot." Even if the vast majority of Americans in 2018 were to want marijuana to be legalized, the only way to change federal law is for the legislative branch to pass new federal laws which the executive branch would then be obliged to enforce. The point is that laws are meant to be obeyed, literally. And if a law is antiquated, then it should be changed. Otherwise, the law becomes a menu from which people simply choose. But few Progressives appear to be able to grasp that sort of logic. At some level, it must be asked: What about that statement do you not understand? Those who do not wish to abide by a given law should be asked to explain why *any* laws should be observed.

starving man? Is it a crime or is it not a crime? . . . If my conscience is the final arbiter . . . I would set him free. . . . But stealing was forbidden by the Almighty . . . whether we understand it or not. . . . Rabbi Akiva maintained that man must not decide solely on his morals and sensitivities, even pertaining to *mishpatim (civil laws)*. . . . This is the basic reason why **secular ethics has failed.** (Soloveichik, *Pesach*, p. 245; bold italics mine)

From Soloveichik's perspective, Gilligan's notion of feminine relational morality is not simply different than a principled morality; the two views are irreconcilable. This distinction separates liberal Progressivism's *unconstrained vision* of morality from Conservatism's *constrained* one.

Where Have All the Men Gone?

Prior to the emergence of feminist movement, the roles of child-rearing and breadwinner were generally divided asymmetrically between parents. In the traditional family, mothers stayed at home to raise children during the day while fathers went to work to provide for their family. But regardless of the configuration, the splitting of roles allowed for the emergence of two distinct voices in child-rearing, although it also created conflicts when parents could not agree.

But this configuration is rapidly disappearing. The divorce rate rose dramatically over the last fifty years, although it recently has begun to stabilize. Many children are currently raised in one parent families, usually by mothers, with little or no opportunities for fathering (C Murray, 1999). According to the CDC data from 2011 to 2013, a high percentage of women ages 25 to 34 (81.6%) agreed with the statement: "It is okay for an unmarried female to have and raise a child" (Statistics, 2014).

Furthermore, many young men have been co-opted by the aims of feminism and the Progressive movement. In their eyes, not to embrace the feminine agenda is *prima facie* evidence of misogyny. As Gilligan notes, if only the traditional male voice is expressed, then softer elements of masculinity are lost. But when only the feminine voice is expressed, there can be little "diversity" of opinions. Rather, the result is a monolithic perspective in which the traditional male voice is neither heard nor desired.

As child-rearing has become increasingly "emasculated," the difficulties that parents experience in setting limits tend to foster the narcissistic entitlement of America's youth (Lukianoff & Haidt, 2015). Even when two-parent families remain intact, there has been a shift in perspective that views parents as contributing "equally" to the nurturing of children, but with both largely assuming the feminine voice.

Traditionally, it was a primary role of fathers to encourage the separation of male children from their mothers. In the past, this was mediated via prescribed rites of passage, but these no longer occur in America with regularity. This leaves young men with few examples of what the masculine voice sounds like, as few outlets for expressing that voice still exist in Progressive households.

Obsessional parenting now has both parents preoccupied with providing a "safe" and "supportive" environment for their children. New parents are hypersensitive to the negative consequences of psychological "micro-traumas" in the lives of their children. The obsessional parent attempts to protect their child *perfectly*. So-called "helicopter parenting" is an amusing term for such a seriously misdirected parenting style.[43] But it is not funny. Mothers, and in many cases, both parents, overprotect their children, intruding into their activities both at home and outside it; they "help" them do what should be *their* children's homework and participate in virtually all their decision making. The child senses the underlying anxieties of obsessional parents and incorporates them via "osmosis." Jung wrote:

The little world of childhood with its familiar surroundings is

---

43 Certainly, obsessional parenting is not limited to America. I recently returned from a trip to Finland, where I heard about "curling" parents. Curling is a sport in which a large stone is slid down the ice with a team of "sweepers" who, with a broom, frantically try to guide the stone to its goal. Different term, same phenomenon.

a model of the greater world. The more intensively the family has stamped its character upon the child, the more it will tend to feel and see its earlier miniature world again in the bigger world of adult life. Naturally this is not a conscious, intellectual process. (Jung, *C.G. Jung, 1962b*)

Motivated by obsessional parents' need to control and fear of making mistakes, the child, rather than becoming independent, instead may become anxious and insecure, failing to develop a "true self," as Winnicott termed it, and ultimately either assume the obsessional style of their parents or rebel against it (DW Winnicott, 1960). In the absence of realistic feedback, appropriate criticism, exposure to reasonable dangers, or the opportunity to experience failure, a child cannot be expected to mature into a healthy, strong, yet flexible adult.

Winnicott recognized that there is no such thing as "a baby," and that it is the dynamic between the infant and caretaker that matters to a child's development. But when the *normal* female narcissism that fosters early attachment to the infant extends well beyond a time when separation is optimally required, the result is a potentially narcissistically disturbed child. This failure to separate proves particularly harmful for male children who ideally at some point need to identify with the male role. But ardent feminists argue against such roles; they prefer that men to be more like women, and women more like men. This approach does not yield an ideal androgyne. Instead, it produces women who feel overwhelmed by attempting to bear too much responsibility, and men who are psychologically emasculated and cannot succeed without maternal support.

We are currently witnessing the results of such disastrous parenting. College students are demanding "safe" zones and insist on being protected from all manner of adversity by university administrators at an age when they should be learning to confront challenges on their own (Lukianoff & Haidt, 2015). Inordinately sensitive to criticism, they exhibit the neurotic immaturity, emotional avoidance, and the inability to make independent decisions. The situation may be aggravated by the continued interference of doting parents who threaten to withhold donations to private universities unless their children's demands are met, and the capitulation of Progressive teachers afraid to confront the ill-conceived demands of students and parents, or who may actually agree with them.

The academic world has been largely co-opted by the Progressive agenda, and university administrators do little to discourage the disruptive behaviors of students who choose to "act out," thereby encouraging more inappropriate behaviors in the future. Progressive educators are apparently unwilling to enforce boundaries or disinclined to force students to confront adversity maturely. As many universities are also dedicated to eradicating the "equality" of meritocracy, including a grading system, hypersensitive students rightly believe that they may have found a comfortable womb in Progressive ideology.

Man-Bashing

Freud referred to "penis envy" as the desire of women to assume what they perceived as the powerful masculine role in society. The concept has been repeatedly attacked by feminists. But it is hard to dismiss in the face of hostile and unjustified accusations leveled at men in recent years by some ardent feminists. Labelling societal problems as the consequence of "toxic masculinity," which is rarely clearly defined, is a strategy aimed at undermining the confidence of young men. Yet political correctness has made it virtually impossible to openly criticize women without being accused of misogyny. In response, men have learned to acquiesce to women and have adopted mannerisms that are excessively soft and not necessarily in their best interests:

A 47-year-old highly obsessional man with Progressive ideas came to therapy because of difficulties maintaining relationships with women. He was careful to be an "empathic" listener and tried hard to intuit their desires in relationship. Despite this, women invariably left him, complaining that he was "too soft." Some treated him overtly sadistically.

Overly compliant men think that it is morally correct to provide their vocal support to feminist causes. Unfortunately, this may include impeaching their own masculinity and accepting the guilt imposed by feminist ideologues for being a "man." They tend to perceive their proper role as being "sensitive." Certainly, integrating feminine qualities into traditional masculine psychology has its advantages, but it is misguided if it expunges all traces of masculinity.

Gender and Bathrooms

The question of what determines gender, nature versus nurture, is complex and currently cannot be answered accurately, but neither is it an arbitrary mystery. The idea that feminine behavior is largely biologically determined and beyond one's control has been vehemently rejected by some ardent Progressive feminists despite scientific evidence to the contrary. They reject the limits imposed by biology, arguing with paranoia that "sex" is a concept adopted by men specifically to control women.

Many of today's feminists support gender-based issues, including homosexuality, same-sex marriage, and the use of public bathrooms by transsexuals in America. In October 2015, the *Chicago Tribune* ran the following news item:

> The battle for equal access for transgender students is pitting Illinois' largest high school district against federal authorities. At issue is locker room access for a transgender high school student in Palatine-based Township High School District 211. The student, who identifies as female, is asking that she receive full access to the girls' locker room. Citing privacy concerns, the district has denied the request and instead offered a separate room where the student can change. "At some point, we have to balance the privacy rights of 12,000 students with other particular individual needs of another group of students," said District 211 Superintendent Daniel Cates. "We believe this infringes on the privacy of all the students that we serve."

But an official with the American Civil Liberties Union, which is representing the student in a complaint filed with the U.S. Department of Education, called the district's stance "blatant discrimination, no matter how the district tries to couch it." Federal officials responded to the complaint, which was filed about a year and a half ago with the Department of Education's Office for Civil Rights, by saying the school is in violation of the Title IX gender equality law, according to the ACLU and district officials.

The proposition that the rights of transsexuals—a minute percentage of Americans—takes precedence over the reasonable concerns of the majority of heterosexuals is mind boggling for some. The definition of sex based on sexual characteristics has been systematically undermined by Progressives, and a new definition based on individual subjectivity has replaced it.

This thinking extends to a host of so-called gender preferences, so that in theory, on any given day, individuals can decide for themselves whether they are heterosexual or homosexual, men or women, or anything in between. Psychiatrists have long recognized that most individuals are located, psychologically speaking, somewhere on a spectrum between heterosexuality and homosexuality, without needing to name the entire spectrum. But the Progressive city of New York currently *officially* recognizes 31 different terms for gender. Based on the patent absurdity of this notion, how is one take the Progressive agenda concerning gender seriously? Yet it is a serious issue, with serious penalties awaiting those who reject it.

The fact that the Obama Justice Department presumed to institute punitive measures against those who oppose the sharing of bathrooms was, to Conservatives, both a moral travesty and an example of interference by the federal government into the private domain. Heterosexuals in Massachusetts who objected to sharing bathrooms with impunity were told by Maura Healey, the lesbian attorney general of Massachusetts, that if they didn't like it they could "hold it." However, on his first day in office, President Trump cancelled the Obama executive order and gave the choice with respect to bathroom rights back to the individual states to determine.

Identity Politics

The convergence of feminism with racial politics has created a "perfect storm" within Progressive ideology. Historically, slavery was the great "sin" of America. Slavery was an established institution at the time of the founding of America, particularly in the Southern colonies, where cheap labor was required for the large cotton plantations. The Founding Fathers were well aware of the problem and reached a compromise that allowed slavery to persist in the South, valuing slaves as 3/5 of a man with respect to representation in Congress. It is often mistakenly believed that this was the result of the racial prejudice of the Founders, when in fact it was the only way that the Northern states could limit the power of the Southern states to legislate the spread of slavery into new territories at the time. Legislation requires compromise and solutions that in their time are judged "good enough." These are not perfect, but they cannot be judged anachronistically by current standards, which is unfortunately what is widely transpiring in America today, spearheaded by those who are either ill-informed lack scholarly historical sensitivity.

Today, few can legitimately argue that substantive progress has not been made on racial issues in America. As David Horowitz notes, "Far from being racists, Americans are the most tolerant people on the planet," and he quotes William H. Frey's statistics from the Brookings Institute as supportive evidence for progress in this regard:

> Sociologists have traditionally viewed multiracial marriages as a benchmark of the ultimate assimilation of a particular group into society. Black-white marriages were still illegal in 16 states in 1967. A 1996 Gallup poll found that only 4% of Americans approved of black-white marriages. Today that number is 87%. In 1960 of all marriages by blacks only 1.7% were black-white. Today it's 12% and rising. (Horowitz, *Big*, p. 25)

When this is considered together with the increased representation of African-Americans in all walks of American life, it's hard to justify why the Progressive left continues to insist that white America is flagrantly racist.

Until recently, women could rightfully view themselves as disadvantaged with respect to men. Consequently, it was not a great leap for the feminist movement to identify with, and to support, the struggles of racial minorities in their efforts at eradicating prejudice. The convergence of feminism with the civil rights movement has been a powerful impetus for the Progressive social justice agenda. Both groups are invested in limiting the influence of American white men. White men who do not cooperate with their demands are "misogynists" and "racists," even when there is no other basis for their claims.

Few women or blacks who are qualified will find themselves rejected out of bias for employment, loans, or other transactions in today's America. Indeed, in many settings, they may find themselves at an advantage with respect to gaining admissions to universities and employment. But qualifications *do* matter, especially for those who are in the business of lending money. If you are unemployed with a terrible credit score, you can expect, like anyone else, to be turned away by a lending institution. If you have no college degree and limited skills, you can expect to encounter difficulties finding a well-paying job whether you are black or white, man or woman.

Furthermore, prejudice cuts both ways. Affirmative action rules that favor certain minorities to the exclusion of others are biased. Whereas affirmative action may have played a necessary role back in the 1960s to jump-start a system that had long been unjust, it is arguably no longer required in a society where institutional prejudice against women or minorities no longer plays a determinative role in the academy or the workplace. Affirmative action policies serve to highlight racial differences and can be biased against non-black minorities. Certain minority groups, most notably Asian Americans, have found themselves penalized for their efforts by seeing what should be merit-based positions awarded to less qualified people of color. In a recent case, aimed at the Supreme Court, the claim was made that Harvard University discriminates against Asian Americans in the service of creating a diverse student body (Harticollis & Saul, 2017):

> The " case asserts that the university's admissions process amounts to an illegal quota system, in which roughly the same percentage of African-Americans, Hispanics, whites and Asian-Americans have been admitted year after year, despite fluctuations in application rates and qualifications.

These biases contribute to the simmering hostilities that plague identity politics.

Furthermore, Progressives, be they white or black, men or women, err in suggesting that *they* are not racists. Some women and black professors openly preach hatred against white men with impunity on university campuses. Efforts to engage them in constructive dialogue are deflected and redirected toward historical grudges against white men. As Horowitz (2017) says:

> The real effect of calling people racists is to drum them out of the company of decent people and to stigmatize them as "extremists, social outcasts and unsuitable to participate in any legitimate conversation. It is because America is not a racist society that racists—at least white racists—are hateful. (Horowitz, *Big*, p. 5)

Psychologically, this is typical of the psychology of envy and victimization. By remaining perpetually aggrieved, victims resist accepting responsibility for their own failures. The fact is that the sympathetic and covertly condescending stance of white liberal Progressives toward blacks has been disastrous for the latter. In large cities sixty years after the Civil Rights Act, many African Americans continue to reside in ghettoes ridden with poverty and high levels of violent crime, most of it perpetrated by blacks against other blacks. Few homes have two parents, and the unemployment rate approaches 50% (C Murray, 1999).

African-Americans, who (based on demographic statistics) had begun to make economic progress in the early twentieth century, when they still lived predominantly in intact families, have (since the institution of the federal Progressive civil rights policies of the 1960s) become increasingly dependent on government welfare support. The result has been the development of a permanent urban racial underclass that no longer participates actively in the workforce and lives with little hope and few economic opportunities, in part due to an educational system that refuses to realistically assess individuals and train them for appropriate employment (C. Murray, 2008).

There have always been children "left behind," as there are real and perhaps insurmountable differences in the intellectual capacities of individuals. Progressive politicians, lacking genuine empathy, have abused urban blacks to suit their political ends, yet many African Americans are not inclined to recognize the harm done to them, as it would require them to assume responsibility for their own future and to shed their grievances against white America for historical injustices that cannot be undone. Real progress and mental health require that aggrieved people mourn their losses and move on, as Freud concluded in *Mourning and Melancholia* (S Freud, 1959b).[44]

Unfortunately, some black Progressive politicians promote anger against whites for their own financial gain. Perennial opportunists such as the Reverend Al Sharpton and Jesse Jackson can be counted on to stir up anti-white and anti-American sentiment amongst African Americans in virtually any situation in which blacks perceive that they have been harmed, even when they may clearly be at fault.

---

44 Religions have recognized this fact, and there are days of mourning that commemorate losses each year helping to ritualize the process. The Jewish fast day of Tisha B'Av commemorates the destruction of the two Jerusalem Temples, but has also over time integrated other great losses. Perhaps a Martin Luther King Day should be observed not merely as a holiday and commemoration of his assassination but a day in which Americans mourn the losses of African Americans over the time that they were enslaved and denigrated in America. This might alleviate some of the resentment that lingers in the black community and inhibits their progress.

One of the extraordinary features of the recent presidential campaign was candidate Donald Trump's offer to raise the standards of urban blacks by providing them with increased economic opportunity. Trump questioned the effects of Democratic leadership on the black community, asking the key question "What do you have to lose?" by shedding the Progressive policies that have produced no tangible economic benefits in America's ghettoes for sixty years. The response by both white and black Progressives was to attack Trump viciously for being a "racist," the label routinely applied to anyone who dares to question the Progressive agenda.

Despite what appeared to be objective progress in racial relations over the last sixty years, Barack Obama appears to have contributed to the deterioration in American race relations. Left leaning quasi-terrorist groups such as Black Lives Matter have foisted a false narrative of persistent prejudice and violence against blacks, one that targets white police. However, as the journalist Heather McDonald documents in the *War on Cops,* evidence to support their claims is impossible to verify (McDonald, 2016). Much of it, like the false narrative that fostered the Ferguson riots in 2015, is fabrication. But President Obama and Progressive leaders, rather than rejecting the factual errors of the radical left, and calling for an end to unprovoked violence against police, instead chose to invite the leaders of Black Lives Matter to the White House as honored guests, signaling their support of violence directed against law enforcement.

No one can deny that there are still bigots and racists in America; that will undoubtedly always be true, in any country, and in all times. But Progressive accusations that America at large is a "racist" country is a lie, and no intellectually honest politician or journalist should lend credence to it.

The city of Chicago has witnessed thousands of murders over the last ten years, with virtually no concern expressed by Black Lives Matter, the mainstream media, ex-President Obama, Progressive politicians, and most notably the mayor of Chicago. Obsessional Progressives have managed to ignore the truth, which allows them to cling to false notions of moral superiority.

Charles Murray poignantly traces the history of identity politics in *Losing Ground* (C Murray, 1984):

Race is central to the problem of reforming social policy, not because it is intrinsically so but because the debate about what to do has been perverted by the underlying consciousness among whites that "they"—the people to be helped by social policy—are predominantly black, and blacks are owed a debt. The result was that the intelligentsia and the policymakers, coincident with the revolution in social policy, began treating the black poor in ways that they would never consider treating people they respected. Is the black crime rate skyrocketing? Look at the black criminal's many grievances against society. Are black illegitimate birth rates five times those of whites? We must remember that blacks have a much broader view of the family than we do and aunts and grandmothers fill in. Did black labor force participation among the young plummet? You can hardly blame someone for having too much pride to work at a job sweeping floors. Are black high-school graduates illiterate? The educational system is insensitive. Are their test scores a hundred points lower than others? The tests are biased. Do black youngsters lose jobs to white youngsters because their mannerisms and language make them incomprehensible to their prospective employers? The culture of the ghetto has its own validity. (Murray, *Losing*, p. 222)

Murray argues that this behavior is nothing less than concealed contempt, supported by a crude psychological denial.

Chapter 13: Mis-Education

The purpose of education is to replace an empty mind with an open one.

—Malcolm Forbes.

Progressivist Pedagogy

Progressivism is a world view with pedagogical goals; its leaders actively seek to instruct the public and educate the young into its ideology. Sowell has referred disparagingly to these Progressive teachers as "self-anointed" seers who believe that *they* know what is best for the future of the country (Sowell, 2011a). Ex-President Barack Obama was as an outstanding example of a Progressive pedagogue. The product of a black underclass, charismatic, articulate, and opinionated, he possessed the qualities that symbolized the new goals of American Progressivism in the twenty-first century.

John Dewey was an early Progressive educator whose methods have influenced public education since the early twentieth century (Watson, 2017). The molding of young American minds has been more successful in recent years than many Conservatives recognize or perhaps allow themselves to concede. Public schools and universities are currently breeding grounds for Progressives, who have been "persuaded" into the correctness of how to speak and behave, and the cardinal importance of racial diversity and multiculturalism in society.

Since the 1960s, it has been increasingly rare to hear Conservative voices on today's college campuses, especially in the elite Ivy League. The degree of Progressive influence on young minds is a concern for those who value differences of opinion and free speech in the marketplace of ideas. The decline of civil discourse on university campuses is not a recipe for the success of liberal democracy.

Fear on Campus

Many young people today are frightened. As journalist Gregg Lukianoff and psychologist Jonathan Haidt note *The Coddling of the American Mind* (Lukianoff & Haidt, 2016):

> Something strange is happening at America's colleges and universities. A movement is arising, undirected and driven largely by students, to scrub campuses clean of words, ideas, and subjects that might cause discomfort or give offense. Last December Jeannie Suk wrote an online article for the New Yorker about law students asking her professors at Harvard not to teach rape law— or, in one case, even use the word violate (as in "that violates the law") lest it cause students distress. (Lukianoff and Haidt, *Coddling*, p. 1)

Hopefully, to many this sounds ludicrous, but it is a genuine problem for those who do not agree with Progressive pedagogy. Consider the story of a patient of mine who is a senior scholar at a local university:

> I can no longer teach want I want. There is little regard for my area of scholarship. The new female chair of my department insists that our curriculum must include subjects that are socially "relevant." Seniority and accomplishment count for nothing. I am afraid to speak up at staff meetings, lest I be criticized or lose my job.

This is an example of the current state of higher education. In addition to the widespread influence of Progressive politics, standards of excellence have deteriorated. As Murray notes, many universities currently offer courses limited to several hours a day, Tuesday through Thursday, with Mondays and Fridays considered "free days." There are no classes on weekends.

There are few introductory survey courses to broad areas of scholarship. Students are free to pick their curriculum and frequently simply search for the least demanding courses required to graduate (C. Murray, 2008). There are virtually no Conservative voices to be heard on many large university campuses, and protests regularly break out when Conservatives like Murray, author Ann Coulter, or the new Secretary of Education, Betsy DeVos, have been invited to speak. A Progressive teacher was physically menaced and injured by students during a protest of Murray's appearance to speak at Middlebury College in Vermont. When subsequently asked who she thought was responsible for her injuries, she responded with the outrageous comment that it was "Donald Trump!" Aggressive Progressive positions on campuses undermine the exercise of free speech, which had traditionally been perhaps the greatest virtue of the academy.

Murray points out that the curriculum of American public schools is currently largely devoid of any substantive content and compares data based on the curricula of public and private schools. The public school curriculum is primarily dedicated to Progressive social justice issues and barely touches on the factual content necessary to educate a young citizen (C. Murray, 2008). A disturbing number of public high school graduates cannot name the vice-president of the United States, do not know what the Supreme Court does, cannot name the capital of Texas, or identify China on a map. In some public schools within the inner cities, the ability to read at what had formerlly been considered a level of competence has been severely compromised. More than half of eighth grade students cannot answer basic simple tests of reading comprehension or reason mathematically. All of what had traditionally been considered required learning has become optional or designed to satisfy the lowest acceptable (C. Murray, 2008). More perplexing is the fact that few appear to be embarrassed by their lack of knowledge or appear to care at all. It is not possible to maintain a credible democracy comprised of illiterate citizens.

A young mother with a young boy in grade school complained to me in therapy that her son had recently come home from school and proclaimed that President Obama was a "great" president because he supported the LGBT community. The mother, who holds Conservative values in a predominantly Progressive community, asked where he had learned that and was told that the teacher had spent the last week discussing how President Obama was protecting everybody's rights in the country. The mother does not share this sentiment and wants her child to be learning facts not propaganda, and she is currently at a loss as to how best to educate her son in Progressive America.

The seemingly benign aims of televised programs for children in the 1970s, including "Sesame Street," "Mr. Rogers," the popular messages of the MTV generation, the widespread availability of escapist video games, and social media pressures, together with an unchallenged Progressive agenda in public and many private schools, have produced a generation of young adults with hypersensitive attitudes about political correctness and distorted perceptions of social injustice. Furthermore, as they are rarely provided with facts and are not exposed to the art of civil debate, they cannot support their opinions and must regress to name calling as a defense when challenged.

"Millennials," who are now coming of age, profess genuine fear of what will happen to them under the new Trump administration. Their fear is regularly witnessed on university campuses and at Hollywood "glitter" events.[45] Their expressions of anger are unquestionably real, but they are unable to explain rationally what the objective basis of their fear is. Instead, attempts at dialogue degenerate into derisive labelling of those who oppose them.

Young people weeping after Trump's election on television appear to be frankly delusional. But this should not be surprising, as they are essentially brainwashed at school and by a relentless Progressive press, and consequently have come to believe that their fears are justified. The

---

45 At a recent event following President Trump's election, Madonna talked about her desire to "blow up the White House." Had that remark been made concerning President Obama or by a non-celebrity, the chances are they might have been interviewed by either the Secret Service or FBI, as well they should be. Remarks like this should not go unpunished or at least should be investigated. Free speech does not extend to making threats against a sitting president without official warning.

mental health community has also been co-opted by Progressivism and political correctness. Therapists have banded together online and in publications to question the mental health of the president. This violates the "Goldwater Rule" of the American Psychiatric Association, which states that it is *unethical* for psychiatrists to make diagnoses without having personally interviewed a person and without their consent.[46]

In some cases, they have taken to the social media to complain about the genuine fears of their patients encumbered by Trump's election while appearing to be unconcerned for others who find their positions equally disturbing. Furthermore, the claim that President Donald Trump is narcissistic is so widely applicable to politicians in Washington, D.C., that one would have to recall virtually all of Congress if that were a criterion for removing politicians from office.

One must question in this age of the "therapeutic" whether young people are being raised to be unnecessarily fearful. There may be nothing more important for the future of America than to address what young students are being taught in our schools. Virtually all religious traditions have recognized that early education is critical in shaping the minds of the young. Fundamentalist religionists would not dream of allowing their children to be "tainted" by the ideas of secular society in a modern public school. In most cases, they will send their children to parochial schools or opt for home schooling, with the desired result. The Jesuit St. Xavier reportedly claimed, *"Give me the children until they are seven, and anyone may have them afterwards."*

John Dewey recognized that the aims of Progressivism would have to be transmitted to the young via government-controlled public education (Nugent, 2010). This represents the major objection that Progressives

---

46 I am old enough to remember the Democratic commercials showing a mushroom cloud and the question of whether Barry Goldwater, the Conservative senator from Arizona, was mentally stable and should be allowed the nuclear access codes. Goldwater lost in a landslide to Johnson, but Congress subsequently adopted a law that it was unethical for mental health professionals to diagnose a politician of standing with a mental disease without having assessed them in person and without their consent.

have toward charter schools and parochial education in this country. The success of Progressivism requires that children be indoctrinated from a young age into its ideology and that the central government retain control of the educational process.

Progressive education is mandated by the federal government to meet goals that reduce focus on the intellectual differences between children. Whereas in earlier times, talented children were promoted to their level of capacity, this rarely occurs today in public schools. Instead, public education is oriented more toward achieving equality in the classroom performance and "ethical improvement" than academic scholarship. School curricula are configured to serve the needs of minorities and those judged as intellectually disadvantaged. Whereas caring for the disadvantaged is an important aspect of public education in a compassionate society, denying genuine differences should not be.

Undoing the Western Canon

The curricula in universities have in recent years progressively devalued the classical canon that had traditionally been viewed as the basis of Western Civilization. It has been rejected as prejudiced toward a "white establishment" (D'Souza, 1991). College courses instead currently focus on black and Hispanic studies, gay and transsexual rights, etc. Achieving racial diversity has become a primary goal of many Progressive academic and business institutions, whether it can be evidentially demonstrated to improve the performance of these institutions or not.

Students are encouraged to adopt values that neither conform to facts nor necessarily serve the future of American society. The idea of American exceptionalism with primacy on the world stage is being systematically undermined by a Progressive agenda that appears to be interested in reducing America's political and economic influence in the world, and serving the economic interests of a globalist elite.[47] Students are taught

---

47 Mr. Obama recently accepted a $500,000 fee for a single speech. That is his right, but how does it jibe with his Progressive concerns about income inequality and the poor?

that America is racist, bellicose, and immoral, rather than the beacon of light that it has been for much of its history. America's young are indoctrinated into a mindset that encourages them to accept guilt for the past wrongs of those who lived in other times and social contexts.

Indeed, one of the most extraordinary transgressions of the current Progressive movement is their willingness to reject historical figures for moral infractions that were widely practiced in their time. Founders like Washington and Jefferson are denounced as "slave holders"; students insist that Woodrow Wilson's name be removed from the Princeton School of Politics for his racist views. Any unbiased historian would condemn the anachronistic applications of current values to individuals who lived in earlier and different times. But liberal Progressive "scholars" appear not to be interested in this basic element of historical methodology.[48]

Obsessional emphasis on minority rights, the bathroom rights of transsexuals, promoting diversity in the armed forces, the American diet, and certain environmental concerns all suggest an extraordinarily narrow vision for America.

None of this bodes well for America's future. Rather than being challenged to think independently, young students are being inculcated into "groupthink." To be fair, education is virtually always a form of brainwashing, as young minds are easily influenced. American children should be educated into the truth. They should not be taught to ignore the misdeeds of their country, as genuine patriotism is not blind. But in the case of America, its misdeeds are balanced, if not greatly exceeded, by its virtues. An objective introduction to American history and governmental procedures, one based primarily on critical historical facts and the function of

---

It is doubtful that he will be providing an honest answer to that question anytime soon.

48 I recognize that certain symbols may be disturbing to minorities in this country. However, they are part of the evolving history of this country. The systematic removal of Southern heroes of the Civil War is no different than the systematic erasures of previous leaders in totalitarian nations. The expunging of memory is part of revisionist history. The death camp at Auschwitz-Birkenau still stands as a reminder of real history and a real Holocaust. How much easier it might be to tear it down.

government and less on the roles of peoples of color or women, would do much to improve the future of young America citizens. There is far more to American history than slavery and misogyny.

Curiously, despite the ubiquitous tentacles of political correctness, young people, when comfortably behind closed doors, manage to watch movies and YouTube videos and listen to music that includes the most vulgar types of misogyny, bigotry, racism, and violence. Something is wrong with this picture. But such paradoxical behavior reflects the obsessional psychology that belies political correctness.

Chapter 14: An Obsessional Elite

The best argument against democracy is a five-minute conversation with the average voter.

—Winston Churchill.

Incestuous, homogenous fiefdoms of self-proclaimed expertise are always rank-closing and mutually self-defending, above all else.

—Glenn Greenwald

Some years ago, I began to encounter a new type of medical student. They were serious young men and women but incapable of accepting even minor criticisms.[49] Although from diverse racial backgrounds, they exhibited a high degree of homogeneity in their previous education and life experience. Most had attended private preparatory schools and Ivy League universities and were now enrolled at Harvard Medical School. Many had taken a "gap year" after graduating college to do volunteer work in Africa, or on Indian reservations, or had worked in a social assistance or education program. They were "good citizens," and their credentials on paper confirmed that. As medical schools are currently essentially closed to anyone without a near perfect academic record and a long list of extra-curricular accomplishments, such resumes surprisingly are not unusual. Professional schools select for overachievers. Some first-year medical students had already developed start-up businesses or made important research findings while working as students in laboratories.

Yet in other respects, these highly talented young people were insulated and immature. They rarely had occasion to associate with others out-

---

49 Saul Alinsky commented that it was critical that political organizers maintain a good sense of humor, another point that eludes the obsessional left.

side of their own elite intellectual and as often socioeconomic class. Even when they had ventured out into the "third world," it had been primarily as observers who knew that they would soon return to comfortable homes in America and continue their virtually guaranteed paths to academic and financial success.

I know a family with two teen-age sons who attended the finest preparatory schools and universities. The family lived at the edge of an ethnically diverse neighborhood, but in a grand house that did not resemble the others in the neighborhood. These two young men were reluctant to venture into the central part of town for fear of encountering working-class people of color, who they judged as "beneath them."

This anecdote sadly exemplifies America's future intellectual elite. They tend to share Progressive ideas, but it is one thing to profess an ideology, another to live it. In *Coming Apart,* Charles Murray poignantly addresses the growth of a distinct intellectual and socioeconomic class in America and the increasing stratification of American society based on intelligence and socioeconomic privilege (C Murray, 2012). The chance for a non-elite young person competing effectively to achieve the American dream is genuinely decreasing.

The young elite learn that it is "good" to champion the causes of the disadvantaged, but they will rarely know who they are or how they live. But that matters less to them than being aligned with the "right" side of the issue.[50] They are "virtue signalers" and do not want to risk being criticized by their Progressive peers.

One cannot overemphasize the fear of being criticized in these young people. One of the pleasures of teaching in the past had been watching gifted students take chances. When asked a question in a group, there used to be a healthy competitive eagerness to "show off" their knowledge. In

---

50   This recalls the issues encountered by George H.W. Bush's failure to have a clue as to how much a container of milk cost when running unsuccessfully for a second term as president in 1992 or Hillary Clinton's carrying around a sample of hot sauce when visiting the African American communities of the South.

one-on-one interactions, students would ask penetrating questions based on their own readings and show a keen desire to learn from their teachers. Virtually all of this is now gone. Questions posed to a group are often met by stony silence and a palpable sense of fear that an incorrect answer will engender shame. Teachers are instead now compelled to provide information didactically, often with little feedback. One-on-one learning opportunities are not much better unless the teacher bends over backwards to make it "safe enough" for the student to respond. Teaching points are often met with a curt "OK," aimed at short-circuiting any further questioning that might discover what they do not know. Consequently, teachers are rarely able to assess accurately whether a student genuinely understands a topic.

The obsessional style of the Progressive scholar is evidenced by the certitude they hold concerning their positions. An example of their shared mentality was revealed in a recent mass e-mailing distributed to the faculty by Drew Faust, the recently retired president of Harvard University, entitled, "We Are All Harvard," in which she attacked the vetting procedures suggested by the new Trump administration directed against seven countries known to be breeding grounds for Islamic terrorism. Following an expression of dismay and anxiety concerning the proposed vetting procedures, Faust wrote:

> I have focused this letter on just a few of the issues and challenges brought to the fore by Friday's executive order and related developments . . . and in an effort to redress inequality, in seeking ways for people with starkly different views to speak and to listen across widening divides, and in striving for a shared commitment to the truth. These and other present concerns are anything but endnotes; they lie at the core of our University.

Unfortunately, the content and tone of her message was anything but an effort to address the "divide" that she refers too, as it included no acknowledgment that there might be faculty members who do not share her opinions, which have become the "official" views of

Harvard and many other academic institutions. There is an assumed homogeneity of thought in academics that isolates and rejects those who do not share their *weltanschauung*. Whereas there have always been political biases in academics and at the workplace, it is only in recent years that official statements promoting ideology have become routine. Professors who used to be "neutral" in the classrooms now insist on injecting their own political views, limit free speech by supporting the "politically correct" agenda, and even stigmatize students who might, with reasoned arguments, disagree with it.

We are witnessing a progressive divide in America based on educational opportunities, socioeconomic status, and political views. An obsessional elite is emerging, and it is positioning itself to determine the future of America without opposition. The greatest threat to a democratic republic is the emergence of an oligarchy whose influence is unchallenged.

Chapter 15: Political Correctness—The Path to Progressive Control

Political correctness does not legislate tolerance; it only organizes hatred.

—Jacques Barzun.

I believe that political correctness can be a form of linguistic fascism and it sends shivers down the spine of my generation who went to war against fascism.

—P.D. James

In a gradual process that began in the 1960s, the United States and much of Western Europe began to embrace a political ideology and behavioral strategy termed "political correctness." The term *politically correct* emerged into the language and culture of the America in the late twentieth century. It was first recorded in William Safire's *Political Dictionary* (Safire, 2008). It became part of the American public debate in the late 1980s, and the media's use of the term was widespread by the 1990s. Political correctness was the label applied to a range of policies in academia, including affirmative action and sanctions against anti-minority speech. A stated goal of political correctness is to revise the traditional academic curricula to reflect the growing emphasis on diversity and identity politics, a trend fostered by the conflation of feminism, gay rights, and racial power politics.

In the journal *American Speech*, Edna Andrews notes that the goal of culturally inclusive and gender-neutral language is based on the concept that "language represents thought" and therefore can be discretely applied to control thought (Andrews, 1996). Janet B. Parks and Mary Ann Robinson validated Andrews's opinion that the language–thought relationship supports the "reasonable deduction ... [of] cultural change via linguistic change" with respect to gender role (Parks & Robertson, 2000). Advocates of "culturally inclusive" language and "gender-neutral" language proposed that such locutions were not optional but mandatory.

The Social Construction of Reality, the seminal text by the sociologists Berger and Luckmann, played an important role in contributing to the development of political correctness (Berger & Luckmann). They argued that both subjective and objective realities are influenced by perspective and as such by both imagined and real events. This is an extension of psychiatrist Aaron Beck's cognitive-behavioral theory, in which perspectives are restructured via cognitions and speech (Beck, 1979).

Political correctness aims at not offending any individual or group in society that is perceived as "disadvantaged." It limits this privilege to people of color, the poor, women, the LGBT community, and religious minorities whom they judge to be persecuted (e.g., Muslims). Asian Americans or Jewish minorities in America are not included in this category, nor are fundamentalist Christians, as they apparently do not meet Progressive ideological standards. But what political correctness truly aims at is controlling ideas and speech that are acceptable to the Progressive state. It is a highly obsessional endeavor.

Although the idea has roots in the sensibilities of the Hebrew prophets and the ethical standards of compassionate Christianity, political correctness outstrips the biblical messages, taking them to extremes that would never have been sanctioned by orthodox religionists. The biblical prophets were charged with confronting the ruling class with unpleasant *truths*, a position antithetical to political correctness, which ignores or denies truths, and instead seeks to quash resistance to its agenda through intimidation.

Political correctness fosters agendas that are not necessarily supported by evidence. "Facts" are declared rather than scientifically proved; challenges to politically correct ideas are met with resistance and hostile epithets. The moral superiority of politically correct ideas is assumed as beyond reproach by those who promote it. Political correctness insists that no real differences exist between men and women, blacks and whites, those who are intellectually capable and those who are not.

The refusal to accept differences, when they suggest that racial minorities are on average at a *real* disadvantage intellectually, through no fault other than circumstances beyond their control (Herrnstein & Murray, 1994), is part of an obsessional strategy that compulsively insists on an ideology of "equality," not evidence. Does this mean that America should give up on those who cannot achieve at the level of others? Absolutely not; but it does suggest that realistically designed educational programs should be offered to lower-achieving young people, rather than trying to fit a square peg into a round hole or holding back those young people who may be intellectually gifted (C. Murray, 2008).

There are a host of collective illusions currently blinding society to the truth. Real differences between the sexes or races are perceived by Progressives through the prism of power. Despite this extraordinarily disingenuous perspective, and its enormous unpopularity in some sectors of society, the politically correct movement has made great strides in Progressive institutions. It has created a self-serving bureaucracy whose role is to disseminate politically correct doctrine and to ensure its application and enforcement. Anyone who has ever been sent to HR for "sensitivity training" can attest to this.

The politically correct movement would force Americans to believe that words are dangerous; that they irreparably injure others; that they will make "racists" and "bigots" of us all unless we carefully censor them. Sensitivity training has become of paramount importance in many of America's institutions. Sensitivity to the feelings of others is a good idea, but when carried to extremes and enforced with punitive actions, one must wonder whether the guaranteed First Amendment rights of American citizens are being routinely violated.

In hospitals, physicians are compelled to take and pass computerized trainings and exams based on mini-seminars created by the administration. The test questions are designed to promote the Progressive politically correct agenda. The following is an actual multiple choice question from a recent "exam."

Question: A patient stops you in the hall to ask directions. You are to:

A. Walk by him because you are in a hurry

B. Stop to give him directions and then go on to your next appointment

C. Direct him to the information booth in the lobby for assistance

D. Stop whatever you are doing and walk him to his destination

If you guessed that the correct answer is "D," you are likely deeply entrenched in the Progressive agenda. But luckily, not everyone is, at least not yet. It apparently does not matter to the PC monitors that a physician might have a clinic full of patients waiting for him, that he is needed in the emergency room, or that he might have to perform a critical surgical procedure. All of this is pales in comparison with doing the politically correct thing.

New and ever-changing terminologies are routinely adopted by the politically correct establishment to expunge potentially discriminatory implications. As Horowitz notes, "Negroes" became "Blacks," then "African-Americans," and then "People of Color" (Horowitz, 2016). But have they changed? The answer is *no*. Changing a name does not change the thing itself. As an ancient Buddhist saying goes, "The finger that points at the moon is not the moon." Those who were previously "crippled" are now "physically challenged," dwarves are "little people," and the list grows ever longer and is ever changing. When a new term is introduced, the older term of speech is reclassified as "hate speech." This has led to a limited backlash from the right, and "political correctness" has become a label for ideas rejected by the political conservatives.

President George W. Bush warned against a Progressive movement that would declare certain topics, expressions, and even gestures "off-limits." A blog by Conservative commentator Ed Kilgore in August of 2015 notes:

> The new era of liberal political correctness—in which colleges designate "free speech zones," words like "American" and "mother" are considered discriminatory, and children are suspended from school for firing make-believe weapons—has reached critical mass.

Even Barack Obama criticized the extremes of political correctness in a speech on September 14, 2014:

> One thing I do want to point out is it's not just sometimes folks who are mad that colleges are too liberal that have a problem—sometimes there are folks on college campuses who are liberal, and maybe even agree with me on a bunch of issues who sometimes aren't listening to the other side, and that's a problem too. I was just talking to a friend of mine about this. You know, I've heard some college campuses where they don't want to have a guest speaker who is too conservative or they don't want to read a book if it has language that is offensive to African-Americans or somehow sends a demeaning signal towards women, and I gotta tell you, I don't agree with that either. I don't agree that you, when you become students at colleges, have to be coddled and protected from different points of view. Anybody who comes to speak to you and you disagree with, you should have an argument with them, but you shouldn't silence them by saying you can't come because I'm too sensitive to hear what you have to say. That's not the way we learn either.

Profound changes in how language is applied *can*, as the political correctness theorists imagined, change how individuals think about interpret their surroundings. But establishing an expurgated common language in society damages freedom of expression. This situation was presented by a prescient George Orwell, who described in *1984* a totalitarian future in which there would be ever-changing dictionaries of socially acceptable "Newspeak" (Orwell, 1950).

There is a tremendous fear of social rejection that people feel when disapproved of, and this is especially true in today's obsessional society. Those who refuse to accept politically correctness can expect to be shunned, ostracized, and risk losing their job; *that* is the truth, and it is frankly frightening for many. Academics who fostered these notions have in some cases fallen victim to how their own ideas have been applied. As Berger (2011) recently noted:

The cultural situation in America today (and indeed in all Western societies) is determined by the cultural earthquake of the nineteen-sixties, the consequences of which are very much in evidence. What began as a counter-culture only some thirty years ago has achieved dominance in elite culture and, from the bastions of the latter (in the educational system, the media, the higher reaches of the law, and key positions within government bureaucracy), has penetrated both popular culture and the corporate world. It is characterized by an amalgam of both sentiments and beliefs that cannot be easily catalogued, though terms like 'progressive,' 'emancipators or 'liberationist' serve to describe it. Intellectually, this new culture is legitimated by a number of loosely connected ideologies—leftover Marxism, feminism and other sexual identity doctrines, racial and ethnic separatism, various brands of therapeutic gospels and of environmentalism. An underlying theme is antagonism toward Western culture in general and American culture in particular. A prevailing spirit is one of intolerance and a grim orthodoxy, precisely caught in the phrase "political correctness."

Unwitting academics like Berger have witnessed how the extreme application of their ideas has led to "grim" results. Burdened by an unremitting perfectionist morality and harsh superego that fails to "take a joke," political correctness parallels the anhedonia of the obsessional. It is a Puritanical endeavor, despite its professed secularism. It is also a totalitarian approach that would in the past have been anathema to Americans, but it is so deeply entrenched currently that it is questionable to what extent its effects can be reversed.

Conclusion:

Everyone in America is soft and hates conflict; the cure for this,
both in politics and social life is hardihood. Give them raw truth.

—John J. Chapman

Having argued for parallels between obsessional apocalyptic psychology
and today's Progressivism, it is necessary to explain why the latter has adopted extreme positions. Many of the reasons have already been touched
upon, and they have been building momentum over decades. But what *is*
new are the digital technologies that have profoundly changed how we
live and who we are. The Internet, smartphones, and social networking
all effectively serve to disseminate ideas. Social networking has increased
psychological pressures to yield to collective thought, what has been pe-
joratively referred to as "groupthink." America is being bombarded with
Progressive propaganda by the mainstream media.

Both Freud and Jung expressed an aversion to the psychology of
groups. The psychoanalytical movement of the early twentieth century
was aimed at fostering individual autonomy and at reducing conformity.
The early psychoanalysts recognized that autonomy was invariably undermined in groups, because as a social animal man is suggestible and easily
influenced by his peers. Freud and Jung lived long enough to experience
the phenomenon of the Third Reich in which masses of otherwise normal
German people embraced virulent ideas and behaviors as a consequence
of a targeted propaganda campaign. Truth was not a consideration, as Hitler realized. People could be convinced by the "Big Lie," as he wrote in
Mein Kampf (Hitler, 1998):

> All this was inspired by the principle—which is quite true within
> itself—that in the big lie there is always a certain force of credibility;

because the broad masses of a nation are always more easily corrupted in the deeper strata of their emotional nature than consciously or voluntarily; and thus in the primitive simplicity of their minds they more readily fall victims to the big lie than the small lie, since they themselves often tell small lies in little matters but would be ashamed to resort to large-scale falsehoods. (Hitler, p. 134)

Communications in groups are complex and include both explicit and implicit elements. Indeed, individuals in groups tend to "synchronize" around certain modes of thought, feelings, and behaviors (C. G. Jung, 1984). This "participation mystique" promotes shared experience of both ideas and actions. Furthermore, people in groups are prone to unstable and irrational behaviors. As Jung said, "Masses are always breeding grounds for psychic epidemics" (C. G. Jung, 1928) para 227). Recently, there have been "spontaneous demonstrations" rapidly organized through social media. This was the organizing medium for the "Arab Spring," and more recently in reaction to the American presidential election.

Enormous numbers of people spend extended amounts of time on Facebook and on other social media (Asano, 2017):

The amount of time people spend on social media is constantly increasing. Teens now spend up to nine hours a day on social platforms, while 30% of all time spent online is now allocated to social media interaction. And the majority of that time is on mobile—60% of social media time spent is facilitated by a mobile device.

This is rapidly becoming the primary modality for communicating with others, and many users also get their news from it. Whether the information is coming from mainstream or digital news networks, it is likely to show bias toward Progressive ideologies, in part because those in the digital communications industry and the so-called tekkies are disposed toward these views. The Internet is in many respects the best example of the *unconstrained vision*, as it resists any sort of regulation or censorship. But paradoxically, ideas offered through digital media are constrained via peer pressures.

The genius of a Mark Zuckerberg, the founder of Facebook, which is the largest social media network, was in recognizing people's yearning for connection in an age of uncertainty. People fear isolation and worry about being socially rejected. For obsessionals, their ambivalence concerning intimate relationships makes social media the ideal mode of communication. Online, one can remain constantly in touch with "friends" without having to interact with them in person. A patient described her experience with dating on social media:

> I've met large numbers of men on-line. I've spent hours messaging with some of them. I enjoy the banter, but I rarely choose to meet with them in person. When I do, I am invariably disappointed. They rarely meet my standards and to be honest, I don't always meet theirs either. But I continue to spend hours "dating" on line. It's better than feeling alone.

This vignette characterizes obsessional relationships in the twenty-first century. Of course, people still meet, marry, and raise families. But for many, social interactions are largely reduced to interacting on Facebook or Twitter, due to their own perfectionism and fears of physical contact and contamination. Social media also allows you to have unlimited numbers of "friends" who are constantly evaluating what they like and don't like about what you are doing or who you claim to be. The social pressure to conform in this "unconstrained" system is enormous.

The recent presidential election proved how powerful these forces are. It was a widely shared "fact," according to polls taken prior to the election, as well as in "exit polls" after the voting, that Donald Trump had "no path" to electoral college victory. This was repeated over and over by pollsters and political commentators on mainstream media. However, ardent Trump supporters continued to suggest that the overwhelming enthusiasm that they had witnessed in person at rallies for their candidate did not jibe with the polling results. When Trump won the electoral vote by a wide margin, the pollsters were forced to admit that they had been wrong. The reasons varied; perhaps they had not sampled a representative audience due to the widespread use of cell phones, etc. But one point kept reemerging in their analysis, and that was that individuals who supported Trump were reluctant to admit it in public, due to fears of being rejected by "friends" in person or on social media. A woman patient who lives in Boston put it to me like this:

> I'm sick of the political correctness and the identity politics. I don't want to share my bathroom with transsexual men. But I keep my mouth shut because all my friends despise Trump and I don't want to be labeled a "bigot" or a "racist" by them, so I say nothing. But I can't wait to vote and I've got my fingers crossed. I'm sick of Obama and his Progressive policies, and I don't think that I'm alone. Trump may even win despite what everyone says.

We may never know for certain what "fooled" the pollsters in this last election, but the above-mentioned phenomenon was apparently widespread. The social pressures induced by the desire not to be rejected by others, to be a "nice" person, and to avoid confrontation, all contributed to a quasi-involuntary muteness by many who held political views that did not conform with those on social media networks.

The most widely consumed ideas are those created by the mass media, including movies, the music industry, and the network news, virtually all of which espouse Progressive values. Hollywood and music industry luminaries have taken it upon themselves to speak up, at times stridently, against Trump and the constrained vision of Conservative Republicans. But with rare exceptions, these "stars" are no more qualified than the average individual to evaluate socio-political issues, but they do take advantage of their fame to assume the bully pulpit. It is difficult to ascertain to what extent their message is influential. By all indications, based on the recent election, it may be highly overrated, but it certainly plays well when preaching to the choir.

Celebrity in politics is a relatively new phenomenon in American society. Indeed, many prominent political figures, including Ronald Reagan, Donald Trump, Arnold Schwarzenegger, and Al Franken, came from the world of show business, where their reputations preceded them. Trump was not only a reality TV star, he was also a successful businessman who had been taking political positions for decades prior to being elected president.

Music is another great motivating force in modern society, particularly for young people. More people currently listen to music, and more of the time, than ever before. The influence of the Beatles and the pop revolution of the 1960s on the nonconforming attitudes of world youth should not be underestimated. The widespread availability of shared music over the Internet has become a way of bonding for young people, and for many it is the most important aspect of their daily lives. The messages conveyed by modern music are varied. The values of hip-hop music are certainly different than those of country music, and their audiences are largely distinct. Their popularities track with the divergent visions of their listeners.

An antinomic and universalist message is conveyed through the lyrics and culture of much of modern rock music. John Lennon recognized the power of popular lyrics and music when he made the controversial statement that the Beatles "were more popular than Jesus," in 1966. Progressive rock tends to undermine conservative values and has been an important factor in doing so. The late John Lennon's lyrics to the song "Imagine" sum it up:

Imagine there's no heaven...no God, above us only sky,
Imagine all the people living for today.
You may say I'm a dreamer, but I'm not the only one,
I hope someday you'll join us and the world will live as one.

This is a call for global secular utopia. Comparable ideas are not being read today in Thomas More's *Utopia*; they are being listened to repeatedly on digital media.

Yet the politically correct movement manages to turn a blind eye to the violent and demeaning lyrics of hip-hop music; lyrics that routinely include the *"N"* word, refer to nonconsensual sexual acts, misogyny, and violence against authority are adopted by the same group that decries any hint of what they judge "offensive" by white Americans. Similar comments can be made concerning the morally high-handed Hollywood elite, whose movies are replete with sex, racism, bigotry, and violence. The apparent hypocrisy of such stances would be laughable if it wasn't both maddening and deadly serious.

Many Conservatives have concluded that Progressives are simply hypocritical liars, and undoubtedly some are, especially those in political positions who are fighting for their political lives. But it is as likely, as Jonathan Haidt (2012) suggests, that many are guided by ideas and feelings that are rigidly fixed about their version of morality, and they won't be challenged by inconvenient logic or facts. But isn't that a definition of delusional mental illness? It certainly used to be.

Failed attempts at cooperative dialogue resemble what predictably happens when attempting to introduce opposing ideas or facts to religious fundamentalists. They will brook no contradictions to their beliefs; they are unconvinced by facts. Whereas they may be fully rational concerning many issues, when it comes to their religious beliefs, all competing rational thought is of no importance. It is an obsessional mindset and one that is dangerously close to what psychiatrists term a "limited" psychosis. But many years ago, it was generally accepted that religious beliefs constituted a protected domain. Should Progressivism or any "ism" be granted that same privilege by law? After all, Progressives in fact closely resemble fundamentalist "religionists," although they have discarded traditional religion. From their view, traditional religion is irrational, but they have replaced it with an ideology that is no less so, because it is essentially also a religion.

As Jung noted (C.G. Jung, 1962a):

Loss of roots and lack of tradition neuroticize the masses and prepare them for collective hysteria. Collective hysteria calls for collective therapy, which consists in abolition of liberty and terrorization. When rationalistic materials hold sway, states tend to develop less into prisons than into lunatic asylums. (Jung, 1962a, para. 282)

Jung's observations continue to ring true for what is occurring in America today.

There has been a breakdown of religious belief and traditional values in America. It has embraced a culture of "therapy," as Rieff refers to it (Rieff, 1966). The obsessional defenses of an overwrought society are beginning to unravel in the face of opposing realities. The daily hyperbolic news broadcasts concerning President Trump's activities are examples of this, and they are leading America nowhere. It would behoove those currently in power to quickly force a legal conclusion to this interminable hysteria, lest the country find itself hopelessly mired for far into the future.

There are obsessional Conservatives who hold extremely rigid views and who inspire conspiracy theories, but their fervency and influence are not as widespread as that of Progressives. This may be because Conservatives are more secure due to their traditional values. Their existential insecurities are contained by law and by the factors of loyalty, respect for authority and the sacred, that Haidt demonstrated in his surveys (Haidt, 2012). The Progressives' reliance on science and humanism offers little emotional comfort. New ideas and technologies can be exciting in youth, but they often tend to tarnish as a source of meaning with age. The challenge to Progressive ideology by Trump's election has left Progressives insecure concerning the future. With no container for their anxieties, violent reactions may emerge.

Currently, political correctness maintains a "polite" reign of terror that divides generations, ethnic and racial groups, religious denominations, obsessionals from non-obsessionals, and has all but paralyzed America. American history is being inaccurately revised with the political aim of emphasizing the positive but historically minor contributions of women and people of color. Comparable strategies have been repeatedly adopted by totalitarian societies.

On a recent tour of Boston's Faneuil Hall, a public historic building dating to the eighteenth century, there were screenings of reenacted Revolutionary War history for curious tourists. But rather than recounting the rich factual history of the times, they all focused on the contributions of African Americans and women. Although both undoubtedly played a role in society at the time, when compared with that of "white men," it was a minor one. But the Progressive goal is not to transmit facts; it is to convey propaganda supporting its moral values.

Revisionist history is a dangerous activity and potentially leads to phenomena such as recent "Holocaust denial." Political correctness and phobic avoidance of anything that might offend undermines proper education while inexcusably politicizing it. Tearing down historical monuments to men whose moral standards may have been applauded in their own time but are no longer viewed favorably is an assault on history and truth. It is a strategy to control the thoughts and memories of a people.

The politically correct movement exhibits the features of obsessional rationalization. It is "rationally" irrational. It declares "realities" that cannot be supported by facts and then contradicts them. It fosters rigid defenses that brook no criticism. Its inability to withstand criticism suggests its underlying fragile basis in deceit, much as the fragile ego of the obsessional is quick to react angrily and defensively.

In a statement to the press in August 2015, Donald Trump declared, "I don't, frankly, have time for total political correctness. And to be honest with you, this country doesn't have time, either." America has traditionally been supported by the spirit of the individual. Americans have espoused non-conformist entrepreneurial attitudes. Despite a credo of respect for others, differences were recognized, critically evaluated, and judged. There was an underlying sense of what was good for America, and when the country was wrong, cooperative efforts were generally made to correct its course.

America has for many years been a multicultural society, a loose confederation of like-minded citizens who shared the values of the dominant society. As Huntington noted, there was a consensual American ethos (Huntington, 2005). But when new immigrants fail to adopt it, one can expect to see profound changes in America.

It is true that powerful nations come and go. Certainly, globalization will likely have a limiting effect on the idea of the nation state and on the exceptionalism of America. It is interesting that the concept of the nation state arose from religious conflict with the decline of the Holy Roman Empire. Globalism is vying to replace nationalism; Progressivism is doing the same with respect to traditional religions. It is possible that Trump's plan to "Make America Great Again" may be merely a temporary interruption in America's inexorable decline. However, it is equally possible that decline may not be inevitable, at least for the immediate future. Restoring national borders, reestablishing individual autonomy, and emphasizing national success could still reverse Progressive trends.

It is not a virtue to have undeterred crime on the streets of a nation. It is not in the best interest of a society at war to allow immigrants from terrorist nations to cross its borders unvetted. The success of America is not fostered when minorities tyrannize the majority, or embrace collective guilt concerning matters that occurred hundreds of years ago. America's youth deserve an education that serves them not only economically but in terms of maintaining the democratic values of the nation. The replacement of traditional religion by fear-driven obsessional systems is not enlightened progress. Progressive ideology as it currently manifests in America is a neurosis. It is neither kind nor compassionate. It aims at repressing truth, replacing harsh realities with utopian illusions.

During the recent presidential campaign, the Democratic partisan Paul Begala made the following remark on the liberal news network CNN:

> Donald Trump's America is fearful. Afraid of crime, afraid of terrorism, afraid of immigrants. His America is angry. Angry about political correctness. Angry about international trade. Angry with President Obama. And very, very angry about Hillary Clinton's candidacy. (Begala, July 26, 2016)

It is difficult to see how confronting problems directly is a failing, but from the perspective of the Progressive left, it apparently is. Furthermore, the anger that this "dark" position evokes in Progressives is difficult to explain, except when it is recognized to be the result of the obsessional defenses of reaction formation and projection. The "dark" view is not a threat to society, as Progressives suggest; but it is a threat to their illusions of security. Freud, who was also accused of having a "dark view" of the world, argued that optimism was an illusion that denied the biological instinctual world and reality (S Freud, 1930). He saw it as part of the obsessional neurosis of mankind.

America can ill afford to remain the highly polarized nation that it has become. It cannot sustain such radical dualism. How to correct this in the future is uncertain, but certain approaches would most assuredly help. Perhaps of foremost importance, political correctness should be expunged and replaced by clear-headed thinking, facts, and free speech, as long as the latter does not infringe on the rights of others. Criteria as to what is or is not psychologically "harmful" are far too arbitrary upon which to base policies. The active enforcement of law must replace what is currently a strategy of arbitrary rulings. If laws are genuinely outdated, they should be removed from the books through the proper processes. Women and minorities must learn how to wield power in ways that do not disadvantage themselves or others. Unfounded accusations against others should be considered libelous, and treated as such, even in the case of celebrities and politicians. The press should be penalized for reporting news that has no basis. Parents should again assume primary responsibility for the education of their children with respect to values, not the federal government.

It should be recognized that obsessionals often harbor deep-seated fears of success and tend to create situations unconsciously that ultimately prove self-defeating. It is my opinion that Hillary Clinton was incapable of "breaking the glass ceiling" because she harbors masochistic fantasies. Her long-standing marriage to an abusive man would tend to support that hypothesis.

Moral masochism allows obsessional Progressives to imagine "loss" as potentially virtuous. Progressives appear to be uncomfortable with the notion of a strong, successful, and competitive America, especially if is associated with aggressive postures. *Virtue signaling*—the conspicuous expression of moral values done primarily with the intent of enhancing one's standing within a social group—has become a popular activity with Progressives. It is the equivalent of the hypocritical religionists who go to great lengths to make public displays of their piety. Jesus described them and warned, "But do not do what they do, for they do not practice what they preach. They tie up heavy, cumbersome loads and put them on other people's shoulders, but they themselves are not willing to lift a finger to move them."

One sees such hypocrisy in statements made by politicians, Hollywood celebrities, and Millennials in their postings on social media sites. They would rather tolerate terrorist attacks and the criminal activities of some illegal aliens, rather than condemn those who perpetrate these acts and take actions to end them, so as not to risk being labeled by others as "racist" or "bigoted." Such individuals have always been present in society, but they are now becoming a force to be reckoned with.

Perhaps the less than totally refined methods of an egotistical businessman president are exactly what the country currently needs if the current Progressive trends in society are to be reversed. If the world can regain an element of stability via clear direct action, rather than ideologically driven speeches, it may help to quell the existential angst that leads to obsessional inaction.

If history has taught us anything about extreme ideologies, it is that they cannot be reasoned with. The only way to deal with a misdirected ideology is to actively and strongly oppose it. Seventy years after the end of World War II, it is worth remembering that nothing stopped the ambitions of the Third Reich or Imperial Japan short of their destruction. In this regard, Americans need to recognize that the recalcitrant ideologies of fundamentalist Islam cannot be reasoned with.

Until law, order, and sanity are restored in this country, the rantings of the Progressive left are certain to become increasingly difficult to contain. One must seriously consider the possibility that they harbor an unconscious goal of destroying the social fabric of this country, perhaps for the sake of profits for economic globalists, and for masochistic reasons, by others. The latter would certainly be my interpretation if a person came to therapy and told me that he or she were consistently putting themselves at a disadvantage in order to be seen as "nice" by others. So why would the same assessment not apply to a society?

Finally, the trend amongst Progressives to devalue their fellow-Americans who hold different opinions must be addressed. This is a sign of apocalyptic thinking in action. There is a disturbing tendency amongst the Progressive elite to dehumanize their opposition. They have come to believe that those who hold opposing views to their own are intellectually and morally inferior and not qualified to determine the future of America. This opinion has no basis in fact, and it is a decidedly un-American mindset unworthy of a great society.

In a magisterial text *Whose Justice? Which Rationality?* the philosopher Alasdair MacIntyre elucidates the critical role of context and tradition in determining what constitutes morality. He argues that ideas derived from different perspectives can be impossible to reconcile via dialogue unless each group is willing to acknowledge the self-consistence of the other. The recognition of history and tradition is critical to any rational approach to morality. Those who "adopt a stance" as MacIntyre argues, requires that:

> Those who adopt the stance become able not only to recognize themselves as imprisoned by a set of beliefs which lack justification in precisely the same way and to the same extent as do the positions which they reject, but also to understand themselves as hitherto deprived of what tradition affords, as persons in part constituted as what they are, up to this point, by an absence, by what is the from the standpoint of traditions an impoverishment. From a Humean point of view they have warped their sentiments in such a way as to render themselves incapable of reciprocity; from an Aristotelian they have refused to learn or have been unable to learn that one cannot think for

oneself...it is only by participation in a rational practice-based community that one becomes rational. MacIntyre, p.396.

In this text, it has been assumed that America's cultural conflicts represent a schism in a secularized version of traditional Judeo-Christian morality. However, that is overly simplistic. Within the Progressive culture, there exist subcultures some of which are minimally bound to any traditional morality. This "far-left" wing of Progressivism is no longer "hierarchical" or "enclaved," as the anthropologist Mary Douglas describes in her schema of societal organization, but instead is best described as "individualistic" or "isolated." The ties of the latter groups to traditional morality are "weak." (Douglas, 2004)It makes little sense to argue with such groups from the perspective of traditional morality because they have dismissed this as no longer historically relevant. Marxist Communism was an example of this, as is radical Capitalism. As Douglas notes, "Each exponent of a cultural bias is acutely aware of threats to the chosen way of life, and so endemic cultural conflict sustains the definition of each culture." (Douglas, p.54) This is where America stands today. Whether transformation is possible remains to be determined.

References

AAP (1994). *Diagnostic and Statistical Manual of Mental Disorders: DSM-IV* (4th ed.). Washington, DC: American Psychiatric Association.

AAP (2017). AAP Statement in Support of Transgender Children, Adolescents and Young Adults [Press release].

Agiesta, J. (2016). Most say race relations worsened under Obama, poll finds. *CNN*. Retrieved from

Alinsky, S. D. (1971). *Rules for Radicals*. New York: Vintage Books.

Andrews, E. (1996). Cultural sensitivity and political correctness: The linguistic problem of naming. *American Speech, 71*, 389-404.

Arendt, H. (1976). *The Origins of Totalitarianism*. Orlando: Harvest.

Ariely, D. (2012). *The (Honest) Truth About Dishonesty*. New York: Harper Perrenial.

Asano, E. (2017). *How Much Time Do People Spend on Social Media?* Retrieved from @mediakix. 2017

Association, A. P. (1994). *Diagnostic and statistical manual of mental disorders: DSM-IV* (4th edn. ed.). Washington, DC: American Psychiatric Association.

Baum, L. F. (1900). *Wonerful Wizard of Oz*. Chicago: Gerge M. Hill.

Beck, A. (1979). *Cogntive Therapy and the Emotional Disorders*. New York: Penguin.

Becker, E. (1973). *Denial of Death*. New York: Free Press.

Bedard, P. (2017). Pew: Trump media three times more negative than for Obama, just 5 percent positive. *Washington Examiner*. Retrieved from Pew Study.

Berg, A. S. (2013). *Wilson*. New York: G.P. Putnam.

Berger, P., & Luckmann, T. *The Social Construction of REality: A Treatise in the Sociology of Knowledge*. New York: Open Road.

Berger, P., & Luckmann, T. (1966). *The Social Construction of Reality: A Treatise in the Sociology of Knowledge*. New York: Open Road.

Bion, W. (1967). Notes on Memory and Desire. *Psychoanalytical Forum, 2*, 1-4.

Bloom, A. (2012). *Closing of the American Mind*. New York: Simon & Schuster.

Bloom, A. (2016). *Republic of Plato*. New York: Basic Books.

Bloom , H. (1993). *The American Religion: The Emergence of The Post-Christian Nation*. New York: Simon & Schuster.

Bowlby, J. (1969). *Attachment and Loss*. New York: Basic Books.

Cannon, W. B. (1932). *Wisdom of the Body*. New York: Norton.

Cohen, S. J. D. (2014). *Maccabees to Mishnah* (3rd ed.). Louisville: W. J. Knox.

Collins, J. (1984). *The Apocalyptic Imagination*. Spring Valley: Crossroads.

D'Souza, D. (1991). *Illiberal Education*. New York: Free Press.

Dallek, R. (2017). *Frankin D.Roosevelt: A Political Life*. New York: Viking.

Damasio, A. (2000). *The Feeling of What Happens*. New York: Mariner.

Dhejne, C., Lichtenstein, P., Boman, M., Johansson, A., Långström, N., & Landén, M. (2011). Long-Term Follow-Up of Transsexual Persons Undergoing Sex Reassignment Surgery: Cohort Study in Sweden. *PLOS, 6*, e16885.

Diagnostic and Statistical Manual of Mental Disorders-V. (2010). Washington: American Psychiatric Society.

Douglas, M. (2004). *In the Wilderness*. Oxford: Oxford University Press.

Eco, U. (1990). *Travels in Hyperreality*. New York: Harvest Books.

Ehrman, B. (2012). *Did Jesus Exist?* New York Harper One.

Erikson, E. (1995). *Young Man Luther: A Study in Psychoanalysis and History*. New York: W.W. Norton & Son.

Ferenzci, S. (1955). *Final Contributions to the Problms and Methods of Psychoanalysis*. London: Karnac.

Fox, J. (2017). One nation of idiots and evil people. *Bloomberg View*. Retrieved from

Frankfurt, H. (2006). *On Truth*. New York: Alfred A. Knopf.

Freud, A. (1962). *Defenses of the Ego*.

Freud, S. (1907). Obsessive acts and religious practice. In J. Strachey (Ed.), *The Standard Edition of the Complete Psychological Works of Sigmund Freud, Volume IX (1906-1908): Jensen's Gradiva" and Other Works, 115-128* (Vol. IX, pp. 115-128). London: Hogarth Press.

Freud, S. (1923). Ego and the Id. In J. Strachey (Ed.), *Standard Edition*. London: Hogarth.

Freud, S. (1924). The Economic Problem of Masochism. In J. Strachey (Ed.), *Standard Edition of the Collected Works of Sigmund Freid* (Vol. 19, pp. 157-173). London: Hogarth Press.

Freud, S. (1927). Future of an Illusion. In J. Strachey (Ed.), *Standard Edition of the Complete Works of Sigmund Freud*. London: Hogarth Press.

Freud, S. (1930). Civilization and its Discontents. In J. Strachey (Ed.), *Standard Edition of the Collected Works of Sigmund Freud* (Vol. 21). London: Hogarth Press.

Freud, S. (1933). New Introductory Lectures. In J. Strachey (Ed.), *Standard Edition of the Collected Works of Sigmund Freud* (Vol. 22). London: Hogarth Press.

Freud, S. (1936). New Outline of Psychoanalysis. In J. Strachey (Ed.), *Standard Edition*.

Freud, S. (1959a). An Autobiographical Study: Inhibitions, Symptoms and Anxiety, The Question of Lay Analysis, and Other Works. In J. Strachey (Ed.), *Standard Edition of the Collected Works of Sigmund Freud* (Vol. 20). London: Hogarth Press.

Freud, S. (1959b). Mourning and Melancholia. In J. Strachey (Ed.), *Standard Edition of the Collected Works of Sigmund Freud* (Vol. 14). London: Hogarth Press.

Freud, S., & Strachey, J. (1989). *Totem and Taboo* New York: W.W. Norton.

Fromm, E. (1960). *Escape from Freedom*. New York: Vintage.

Garrow, D. (2017). *Rising Star*. New York: Amazon Digital Services.

Gerlernter, D. (2007). *Americanism*. New York: Doubleday.

Gilligan, C. (1999). *In a Different Voice*. Cambridge: Harvard University Press.

Goodwin, D. K. (1991). *Lyndon Johnson and the American Dream*. New York: St. Martin's Griffin.

Gray, J. (2012). *Men are from Mars , Women are from Venus*. New York: Harper.

Habermas, J. (1981). *The Theory of Communicative Action*. Boston: Beacon Press.

Habermas, J., & Ratzinger, J. (2006). *The Dialectics of Secularization*. San Francisco: Iganatius.

Haidt, J. (2012). *The Righteous Mind: Why Good People are Divided by Politics and Religion*. New York: Pantheon Books.

Hall, C. (1999). *Primer of Freudian Psychology*. New York: Plume.

Hanson, P. (1979). *The Dawn of Apocalyptic*. Philadelphia: Fortress Press.

Harticollis, A., & Saul, S. (2017). Affirmative Action Battle Has a New Focus: Asian-Americans. *N,.Y. Times*.

Hegel, G. W. F. (2016). *Elements of the Philosophy of the Right*. Cambridge: Cambridge University Press.

Herrnstein, R. J., & Murray, C. (1994). *The Bell Curve*. New York.

Hitler, A. (1998). *Mein Kampf*. New York: Houghton Mifflin Company.

Holmes, K. (2016). *Closing of the Liberal Mind: How Groupthink and Intolerance Define the Left*. New York: Encounter Books.

Horowitz, D. (2004). *Unholy Alliance*. Washington, DC: Regenery Publishing.

Horowitz, D. (2016). *Progressive Racism*. New York: Encounter Books.

Huntington, S. (2005). *Who Are We?* New York: Simon & Schuster.

Ingram, I., & May 1961, -. Obsessional Illness in Mental Hospital Patients. *The British Journal of Psychiatry, 107*.

Janet, P. (1921). *Fear of Action.* Retrieved from Atlantic City:

Jung, C. G. (1928). Development of Personality. In H. Read, M. Fordham, & G. Adler (Eds.), *Collected Works of C.G. jung* Vol. 17). Princeton: Bollingen/Princeton.

Jung, C. G. (1950). *Modern man in search of a soul.* New York,: Harcourt.

Jung, C. G. (1962). Introduction to Secret of the Golden Flower *(Collected Works of C.G. Jung,* (Vol. 13). Princeton: Princton Univerity Press.

Jung, C. G. (1962a). The Psychogenesis of Mental Disease. In H. Read, M. Fordham, & G. Adler (Eds.), *Collected Works of C.G. Jung.* Princeton: Bollingen/Princeton.

Jung, C. G. (1962b). The Theory of Psychoanalysis In H. Read, M. Fordham, G. Adler, & W. McGuire (Eds.), *Collected Works of C.G. Jung* (Vol. 14). Prinecton: Princeton/Bollingern.

Jung, C. G. (1970). *Aion: Researches into the Self* (Vol. 9). Princeton: Princeton Univeristy Press.

Jung, C. G. (1984). *Psychology of Religion: West and East.* Princeton: Princeton University.

Jung, C. G. (1998). *Jung on Myth.* Princeton: Princeton University Press.

Jung, C. G., & Jaffe, A. (1959). *Memories, Dreams, Reflections.*

Jung, E. (1985). *Anima and Animus.* Dallas: Spring.

Jung, E., & von Franz, M. (1998). *The Grail Legend.* Princeton: Princeton/Bollingen Press.

Kano, M., Mizuno, T., Kawano, Y., Aoki, M., Kanazawa, M., & Fukudo, S. (2012). Serotonin transporter gene promoter polymorphism and alexithymia. *Neuropsychobiology., 65,* 76-82.

Kant, I. (1780). *Critique of Pure Reason*. London: Longmans, Green & Co.

Katz, S. T. (1992). *Mysticism and Language*. New York: Oxford University Press.

Kernberg, O. (1995). *Borderline Conditions and Pathological Narcisssm*. Northvale: Jason Aronson.

Keyes, R. (2016). *The Post-Truth Era: Dishonesty and Deception in Contemporary Life*. New York: St. Martins Press.

Klein , J. (2002). *The Natural: The Misunderstood Presidency of Bill Clinton*. New York: Doubleday.

Klein, M. (1958). Development of mental functioning. In F. Press (Ed.), *Envy and Gratitude;The Writings of Melanie Klein*. New York: Free Press.

Koh, M., Kang, J., Namkoong, K., Lee, S., & Kim, S. (2016). Association between the Catechol-O-Methyltransferase (COMT) Val[158] Met Polymorphism and Alexithymia in Patients with Obsessive-Compulsive Disorder". *Yonsei Medical Journal, 57*, 721-727.

Kradin, R. (1999). Generosity: a psychological and interpersonal motivational factor of therapeutic relevance. *J Anal Psychol, 44*(2), 221-236.

Kradin, R. (2007). Minding the Gaps:

The Role of Informational Encapsulation and Mindful Attention in the Analysis of Transference. *Journal of Jungian Theory and Practice, 1*, 1-13.

Kradin, R. (2008). *The Placebo Response*. New York: Routledge.

Kradin, R. (2016). *Parting of the Ways*. New York: Academic Studies Press.

Kradin, R., & Benson, H. (2000). Stress, the relaxation response and immunity. *Mod Asp Immunobiol, 1*, 110-113.

Kradin, R. L. (1997). The psychosomatic symptom and the self: a sirens' song. *J Anal Psychol, 42*(3), 405-423.

Kradin, R. L. (2004). The placebo response: its putative role as a functional salutogenic mechanism of the central nervous system. *Perspect Biol Med, 47*(3), 328-338.

Krakauer, J. (1999). *Into Thin Air*. New York: Anchor.

Kristol, I. (1995). *Neoconservatism: The Autobiography of an Idea*. New York: Simon & Schuster.

Kurtz, H. (2018). *Media Madness:Donald Trump,Media Madness and the War Over Truth*. New York: Regnery.

Kwong, J. (2018). *Trump is the Worst President, Export Ranking Survey Reveals on Presidents Day, Newsweek* [Press release]

Lakoff, G. (2016). *Moral Politics*. Chicago: University of Chicago Press.

Lasch, C. (1979). *The Culture of Narcissism: American Life in an Age of Diminishing Expectations*. New York: W.W. Norton.

Lau, M. (2007). *A Comprehensive Commentary on Ethics of the Fathers*. New York: Mesorah.

Lifton, R. J. (2000). *The Nazi doctors : medical killing and the psychology of genocide : with a new preface by the author* (2000 ed.). New York: Basic Books.

Liptak, A. (2017, December 4). Supreme Court Allows Trump Travel Ban to Take Effect. *N.Y. Times*.

London, P. (1986). *The Modes and Morals of Psychotherapy* (2nd ed.): Routledge.

Lukianoff, G, & Haidt, J. (2015). Coddling of the American Mind. *Atlantic*.

Mac Intyre, A. (2007). *After Virtue* (3rd ed.). Notre Dame: Notre Dame Press.

Marx, K., & Engels, F. (2014). *The Communist Manifesto*. New York: International Publishers.

McDonald, H. (2016). *The Wars on Cops*. New York: Encounter Books.

Meeks, W. (1993). New Haven: Yale University Press.

Mehring, F. (2003). *Karl Marx: The Story of His Life*. London: Routledege.

Murray, C. (1984). *Losing Ground*. New York: Basic Books.

Murray, C. (1999). *The Underclass Revisited*. Washinton, DC: AE!

Murray, C. (2008). *Real Education*. New York: Cox and Murray.

Murray, C. (2012). *Coming Apart*. New York: CrownForum.

Neusner, J., & Chilton, B. (Eds.). (2009). *The Golden Rule*. Latham: University Press.

Newport, F. (2015). Percentage of Christians in U.S. Drifting Down, but Still High. *Gallupnews*. Retrieved from

Nietsche, F. (2017). *The Essential Nietzsche: Beyond Good and Evil and The Genealogy of Morals*. London: Chartwell.

Nisbet, R. (1969). *Social Change and History*. Oxford: Oxford University Press.

Norenzayan, A. (2013). *Big Gods: How Religion Transformed Cooperation and Conflict*. Princeton: Princeton Univerity Press.

Nugent, W. (2010). *Progressivism: A Very Short Introduction*. Oxford: Oxford.

O'Neill. (2017). Commentary: What happened to 'innocent until proven guilty'? *Chicago Tribune*. Retrieved from

Ogden, T. (2005). *Projection and Psychotherapeutic Technique*. London: Karnac.

Orwell, G. (1950). *1984*. New York: Penguin.

Parks, J. B., & Robertson, M. A. (2000). Development and Validation of an Instrument to Measure Attitudes Toward Sexist/Nonsexist Language. *Sex Roles, 42*, 415-438.

Pediatrics, A. A. o. (2017). AAP Statement in Support of Transgender Children, Adolescents and Young Adults [Press release]

Piaget, J. (1960). *The Psychology of the Child*. New York: Basic Books.

Prestigiacomo, A. (2016). Former Johns Hopkins psychiatrist blasts transgender movement. *The Dailywire*.

Reavis, D. (1995). *The Ashes of Waco:An Investigation*. Syracuse: University of Syracuse.

Reich, W. (1962). *Character Analysis*. New York. Farrar, Straus and Giroux.

Rich, J. (2007). *Modern Feminist Theory: An Introduction*

Rieff, P. (1966). *Triumph of the Therapeutic*. Chicago: University of Chicago Press.

Rieff, P. (1979). *Freud: Mind of Moralist*. Chicago: University of Chicago.

Rossi Neto, R., Hintz, F., Krege, S., Rübben, H., & vom Dorp, F. Gender reassignment surgery - a 13 year review of surgical outcomes. *International Brazilian J. Urology, 38*, 1677.

Safire, W. (2008). *Political Dictionary*. Oxford: Oxford University Press

Salzman, L. (1977). *Treatment of the Obsessional Personality*. Northvale: Jason Aronson.

Sapolsky, R. (2017). New York: Penguin Press.

Sartoru, S. (2016). Alexithymia: The Emotional Disconnect Behind the Mask of Normalcy. Retrieved from Nippon.com

Schama, S. (1990). *Citizens: A Chronicle of the French Revolution*. New York: Vintage.

Scholem, g. (1995). *The Messianic Idea in Judaism*. New York: Schocken.

Schwarz, H. S. (2003). *Revolt of the Primitive*: Transaction Publishers.

Shapiro, D. (1981). *Autonomy and Rigid Character*. New York: Basic Books.

Shoemaker, K. (2011). *Sanctuary and Crime in the Middle Ages*. New York: Fordham University Press 284 pp.

Sifneos, P. (1996). Alexithymia:Past and present. *American Journal of Psychiatry, 22*, 255-262.

Sims, A. (2003). *Paul Ricouer*. London: Routledge.

Smith, J. (2016). *Bush*. New York: Simon & Schuster.

Sowell, T. (2007). *A Conflict of Visions*. New York: Basic Books.

Sowell, T. (2011a). *Intellectuals and Society*. New York: Basic Books.

Sowell, T. (2011b). *The Thomas Sowell Reader*. New York: Basic Books.

Spitzer, R., Vol. 32, No. 5, October 2003: 403-417. (2003). Can Some Gay Men and Lesbians Change Their Sexual Orientation?". *Archives of Sexual Behavior,, 32*, 403-417.

Statistics, N. V. (2014). *National Marriage and Divorce Rate Trends 2000-2014*. Atlanta: US Government.

Stern, D. N. (1985). *The Interpersonal World of the Infant*. New York: Basic Books.

Storm, I. (2015). Morality in Context: A Multilevel Analysis of the Relationship between Religion and Values in Europe Politics and Religion. *Politiics and Religion, 1*, 28.

Stoyanov, Y. (2000). *The Other God*. New Haven: Yale University Press.

Strauss, L. (1953). *Natural Right and History*. Chicago: University of Chicago.

Strozier, C. (2001). *Heinz Kohut: The Making of a Psychoanalyst*. New York: Farrar Straus Giroux.

Sulloway, F. (1979). *Freud: Biologist of the Mind*. New York: Basic Books.

Summers, L. (2016) *Conversations with Bill Kristol/Interviewer: B. Kristol*. Conversations with Bill Krystol.org.

Szasz, T. (2010). *Myth of Mental Illness*. San Francisco: Harper Perrenial.

Tomasello, M. (2016). *Natural History of Morality*. Cambridge: Harvard University Press.

Valdassalo, J. (2015). Fixing the Problem of Liberal Bias in Social Psychology. *Psychology Today*.

Vanheule, S., Desmet, M., Meganck, R., & Bogaerts, S. (2007). Alexithymia and interpersonal problems *Journal of clinical psychology, 63*, 109-117.

Vermes, G. (2012). *Complete Dead Sea Scrolls in English*. New York: Penguin.

von Franz, M. (1985). *Projection and Re-collection in Jungian Psychology*. London: Open Court Publishing.

Watson, B. C. S. (2017). *Progressive challenges to the American constitution : a new republic*. Cambridge, United Kingdom ; New York, NY: Cambridge University Press.

Weber, M. (2002). *The Protestant Ethic and the Spirit of Capitalism: and Other Writings*. New York: Penguin Books.

Weisberg, Y., DeYoung, C, & Hirsh, J. (2011). Gender Differences in Personality across the Ten Aspects of the Big Five. *Frontiers in Psychology, 2*, 178-185.

Wells, H. G. (2004). *The Outline of History* (Vol. One). New York: Barnes and Noble.

Wells, H. G. (2016). *The Time Machine*.

Winnicott, D. (1960). *The Maturational Process and the Facilitating Environment*. New York: International Universities Press.

Winnicott, D. (1966). Maternal Preoccupation. In P. Mariotti (Ed.), *Identification, Desire, and Transgenerational Issues*. East Sussex: Routledge.

Yerushalmi, H. (1996). *Zachor*. Seattle: University of Washington Press.

Index